Tools

English joiners, painted in 1816 by George Forster (?–1842),
oil on canvas, England. Many early American woodworkers
labored in similar environments. Courtesy of the private
collection of Barry and Carol Eisenberg, in memory of
Bernard H. Taff.

Tools

Working Wood
in Eighteenth-Century America

By
James M. Gaynor
and
Nancy L. Hagedorn

The Colonial Williamsburg Foundation
Williamsburg, Virginia

Library of Congress Cataloging-in-Publication Data

Gaynor, James M.
    Tools : working wood in eighteenth-century America / by James M. Gaynor and Nancy L. Hagedorn.
        p.   cm. — (Wallace Gallery decorative arts publications)
    Includes bibliographical references and index.
    ISBN 0-87935-098-9
    1. Woodworking tools—United States—History—18th century.
    2. Woodworking tools—England—History—18th century. I. Hagedorn, Nancy L. II. Title. III. Series. IV. Series: Wallace Gallery decorative arts publication.
    TT186.G39 1993   93–31754
    684'.082'097309033—dc20   CIP

Book design: Vernon Wooten

Printed and bound in Canada

Colonial Williamsburg photography by Hans Lorenz and Craig McDougal
Cover photograph by Tom Green and Lael White
Front cover: Hay's Cabinetmaking Shop at Colonial Williamsburg.
Back cover: Gentleman's tool chest sold in London in 1773.

Williamsburg Decorative Arts Series

Graham Hood, *Editor*

For Dad. — JMG

In memory of Grandpa Parker, who could fix anything and taught me to appreciate what tools could do in the right hands, and to my parents for their constant love and support. — NLH

Contents

Foreword

As a museum with the avowed aim of representing an entire colonial city over several decades, Colonial Williamsburg has long placed an emphasis on the important infrastructure of work in that society. Available work was one of the great opportunities of the New World. Most work required some kinds of tools, and as this continent offered seemingly limitless supplies of timber, it was inevitable that many of the tools should be specially designed to shape that material. Thus the eighteenth century's dependence on and need for tools to fashion wood has been reflected in the collecting policies of this museum.

Many museum goers who love furniture and architecture and who linger to admire their myriad exquisite details rarely consider the refined tools that made such artistry possible. The skill and judgment of the hand and the eye of cabinetmaker, carver, and joiner are sometimes regarded with awe, but rarely their tools, which in fact were often designed and made with comparable expertise. The exhibition, of which this book is a record, attempts to redress that balance and to show Colonial Williamsburg's important collection of eighteenth-century tools, along with selected examples from other public and private collections. It is, to our knowledge, the first time a tool exhibit of this scope has been presented in an art museum in this country. It seeks to show tools as dynamic things, designed to create, an important component of a developing technology and a burgeoning mercantile economy. And it reveals how old tools, through their wear and patina, can take the mind quickly back to the people whose livelihood depended on them and in whose lives tools played such a vital role.

This unusual exhibit is the brainchild of James M. Gaynor, curator of mechanical arts at Colonial Williamsburg, as is the book. Jay has toiled with all the fortitude, skill, and determination of one of the ancient craftsmen he so admires to bring both into being. Nancy L. Hagedorn, project research historian, worked with Jay on nearly every aspect of the book and exhibit and contributed her considerable skills to their realization. In addition, a host of Colonial Williamsburg's staff, volunteers, contractors, the staffs of sister institutions, and private researchers and collectors have given much and are acknowledged in the pages that follow. We are very grateful to so many for their dedication to these often overlooked but vital artifacts and for their commitment to sharing them with the Colonial Williamsburg Foundation's diverse audience.

Graham Hood
Vice President, Collections and Museums
Carlisle H. Humelsine Curator

Preface

This book was written to accompany an exhibit of the same title presented at the Colonial Williamsburg Foundation's DeWitt Wallace Decorative Arts Gallery from January 1994 through June 1995. The exhibit was made possible in part by a planning grant from the National Endowment for the Humanities, a federal agency. While the book summarizes and elaborates upon many of the exhibit themes and illustrates many of the objects included in the exhibit, it is intended to be equally useful to those who have visited the exhibit and those who have been unable to do so. We have designed it to be an introduction to eighteenth- and very early nineteenth-century woodworking tools for those with a general interest, novice collectors, and woodworkers who want a bit of information about the history of their tools. We also have included many never before published illustrations of early tools, information about early makers, and tool history that we hope will interest those with more advanced knowledge.

We have relied heavily upon the work of other historians, tool collectors, and museum curators. Numerous books and articles, many of which are included in the reading list, explore the topics of woodworking hand tools, their makers, and their users. Many of these treat technical topics and specific uses and users, most frequently those of the nineteenth century, in detail. We heartily recommend them to you if this book inspires a quest for more information.

We hope the contribution of this book is its focus upon the tools of an earlier period and its broad consideration of woodworking tools as objects that reflect the times in which they were made and used. We believe tools are an important window through which to view and understand many aspects of life in eighteenth-century America. Hence our purpose has been to present not so much a detailed technical discussion, but rather a summary overview of how these tools came to be, how their users acquired and learned to use them, and how they influenced the working lives and products of woodworking artisans. In presenting this story, we have concentrated on Virginia. We also discuss English tool manufacturing and marketing as well as toolmaking and use in other regions of America in order to place the role of tools in Virginia within a larger economic and cultural context.

The book is divided into two sections. The first is a discussion about the origins of tools, their manufacture, acquisition, and use. The second is a pictorial essay exploring five basic tool types: measuring and marking tools, chisels and gouges, saws, tools for boring holes, and planes. If the reader is not familiar with basic tools and their uses, we recommend that he or she start with the second section. A glossary of technical terms will be found near the end of the book.

A comment is in order regarding our dating of tools and makers. Dates given are normally those during which the maker (or a related company) is documented as working. Because surviving sources of such information give only sporadic coverage for the period—the earliest available Birmingham city directory, for example, was published in 1767; the earliest Sheffield directory in 1774—the dates we give are not necessarily the actual beginning and ending working dates of the maker. He or she could have been working earlier or later than indicated. Many of the working dates of toolmakers have been derived from our own research, much of it from contemporary English city directories. We have also drawn on the published work of Kenneth Roberts, William L. Goodman, Emil and Martyl Pollak, and Elmer Z. Longenecker.

Finally, in an effort to make the book more accessible to the casual reader, the decision was made to limit endnotes primarily to direct quotations. Unless indicated otherwise, catalog numbers are for tools from the Colonial Williamsburg collection. Since most of the tools have survived long working lives, many have replaced handles or blades fitted while the tools were in use or in the course of more recent restoration. Unless we believe replacements and restorations significantly modify the original appearance of the tools, we have not noted these alterations.

We hope you enjoy your foray into the world of old tools.

Acknowledgments

Neither this book nor the exhibit it accompanies would have been possible without the support, encouragement, assistance, and hard work of many individuals and institutions. Mentioning them here seems paltry thanks, but we ask each of them to realize that behind these words is a world of heartfelt appreciation for their faith in our work; their unstinting generosity with their knowledge, collections, and financial support; their sharing of talents and skills; and the long hours and inconveniences they endured to bring these efforts to fruition.

The tool study project and resulting exhibit and book owe their existence to the strong commitment of the Colonial Williamsburg Foundation and the support of the National Endowment for the Humanities, which awarded the exhibit a planning grant. In addition, several individuals made generous financial donations at the outset of the project: Mr. and Mrs. Roger Clapp, Mr. and Mrs. Clair H. Gingher, Jr., and Mr. and Mrs. Emil Pollak. They gave their support when all of this was little more than a curator's dream. Mr. and Mrs. Victor Cole and a matching gift from United Technologies Corporation also aided the project.

Among those who have given of their time and talents, we must begin by thanking Graham Hood, vice president of collections and museums, and Jan Gilliam, assistant curator. Graham has been a believer in this project from its inception and championed its purposes and progress unfalteringly. Jan has worked with us tirelessly in nearly every undertaking and has given us a constant breath of fresh air, a bright smile, and truly creative insights.

Aline Landy, DeWitt Wallace Decorative Arts Gallery exhibits manager, coordinated the many phases of exhibit production. Rick Hadley, exhibit designer, transformed the shelves of tools and our often nebulous concepts into a striking reality. Don Thomas oversaw aspects of Gallery administration and programming. Working with them were Wallace Gallery exhibit staff members Gayle Trautman and Gloria McFadden. Brenda LaClair, museum educator, played a crucial role in the development of exhibit educational programs. From outside the Foundation we drew on the graphic design skills of XY&i of Washington, D. C.

Donna Sheppard, editor extraordinaire, ironed out many of the creases in our manuscript and labels. Vernon Wooten designed this book. Robin Reichner Franklin did many of the drawings that appear in both the book and exhibit. Louis Luedtke prepared the map.

All members of the Collections Department got into the act at some point. Individual curators helped with object selection and information about their collections, and provided fresh perspectives regarding the manuscript. Martha Katz-Hyman took over many of Jay's daily curatorial duties, freeing him to concentrate on the project. Hans Lorenz, Craig McDougal, Lauren Suber, and volunteer Paul Knox have conjured the magic of their photo studio, managed the complexities of scheduling, and sorted and filed countless images to create and make available most of the illustrations in this book and many of the exhibit graphics. Margie Gill, Kim Smith Ivey, Robert Jones, Linda Wilson, and volunteers Rebecca Fass, Carol Harrison, and John Willis handled the mound of paperwork involved in loans and made sure record photos were taken. Curatorial intern Ellen Fitzgibbons conducted a visitor survey, helped with the research, and, with the aid of volunteer David Westpfahl, cataloged many of the exhibit objects. Intern Steve Dortch undertook documentary research. Davelin Forrest and Velva Henegar ordered supplies, paid bills, answered myriad questions, and, most important, made sure we all got paid.

Conservators Steve Ray, Harold Gill III, J. P. Mullen, David Harvey, Linda Vrooman, Carey Howlett, Albert Skutans, Leroy Graves, and Loreen Finkelstein, with the aid of interns Clinton Fountain, Kathy Gillis, Len Hambleton,

Joanna Harris, Linda Landry, and Dylan Smith, and volunteers Trip Kahn, Jack Teasley, and William Potts, cleaned and restored hundreds of objects for photography and the exhibit.

Many other Colonial Williamsburg staff members also lent their skills and experience to creating the book and exhibit. Robert Birney, Steve Elliott, Wallace Gusler, Lawrence Henry, Mike Kipps, Richard McCluney, Dennis O'Toole, Joseph Rountree, Beatrix Rumford, John Sands, and Carolyn Weekley gave unstintingly of their support and administrative abilities to keep the project moving forward. Ann Smart Martin assisted us with documentary research and provided many insights. Susan Shames and John Ingram answered numerous questions and helped us obtain needed library materials. Ken Kipps handled exhibit publicity. Conny Graft and Mark Howell helped us to keep our educational goals firmly in sight and to remember our audience. Mike Durling, Mary Economou, Mike Puckett, Chuck Smith, and Jim Survil, with the assistance of Pete Roberts, Jamieson Redd, and Scott Lage, worked their audiovisual magic. Tom Green and Lael White photographed the cover of this book and many of the graphics appearing in the exhibit. Rebecca Rhyne, Bonnie Penney, and Jan Bennett spearheaded the development of special exhibit-related products. John Hamant and Deborah Chapman of Special Programs were instrumental in planning special events. Annie Davis, Sarah Houghland, Albert Louer, and Sharon Thelin helped with grant applications and development efforts. Carl Lounsbury, Willie Graham, and Mark R. Wenger of Architectural Research, Kevin Kelly of Historical Research, Bill Pittman of Archaeological Research, and Mike Lewis of the Museums Division were always available to answer questions, no matter how strange.

Artisans of the Division of Historic Trades made many aspects of the exhibit possible. Cornelius Black, Roy Black, John Boag, Shelton Browder, Jay Close, Brian Evans, Richard Guthrie, Marcus Hansen, Mack Headley, Jon Laubach, Lew LeCompte, Bill Little, Kaare Loftheim, Steve Mankowski, Heather McCoy, Dick Peeling, George Pettengell, Jim Pettengell, Bruce Plumley, Noel Poirier, Wayne Randolph, Michael Rhodes, Peter Ross, Tim Russell, David Salisbury, Kenneth Schwarz, Kerry Shackelford, Felix Simmons, Jim Slining, Jim Townsend, Ron Vineyard, Bill Weldon, George Wilson, Garland Wood, Christopher Wright, and Edward Wright produced many of the reproduction tools and products for the exhibit, posed and worked in front of cameras for exhibit photography, and provided a wealth of technical information and advice. Ken Schwarz coordinated production by these artisans, and Mack Headley served as the official Historic Trades representative on the exhibit planning committee. These individuals are just the tip of the iceberg. As the exhibit and related events are implemented, many other Colonial Williamsburg departments and staff will contribute their efforts.

Numerous institutions both here and in England have lent objects or provided photographs, allowing us to include their treasures in the book and exhibit: Birmingham Central Library and Archives, Birmingham, Eng.; Birmingham Museums and Art Gallery, Birmingham, Eng.; British Museum, London, Eng.; James Duncan Phillips Library, Peabody and Essex Museum, Salem, Mass.; Earl Gregg Swem Library, College of William and Mary, Williamsburg, Va.; The Farmers' Museum, Cooperstown, N. Y.; Flowerdew Hundred Foundation, Hopewell, Va.; Framingham Historical and Natural History Society, Framingham, Mass.; Guildhall Museum, Rochester, Kent, Eng.; Henry Francis du Pont Winterthur Museum, Winterthur, Del.; Jamestown Settlement and Yorktown Victory Center, Jamestown-Yorktown Foundation, Williamsburg, Va.; John Carter Brown Library, Brown University, Providence, R. I.; Kelham Island, Sheffield City Museum, Sheffield, Eng.; Library of Congress, Washington, D. C.; Maryland Historical Society Library, Baltimore, Md.; Mary Rose Trust, Portsmouth, Eng.; Mercer Museum, Bucks County Historical Society, Doylestown, Pa.; Metropolitan Museum of Art, New York, N. Y.;

Mount Vernon Ladies' Association, Mount Vernon, Va.; Museum of Early Trades and Crafts, Madison, N. J.; Museum of London, London, Eng.; National Museum of American History, Smithsonian Institution, Washington, D. C.; National Museums & Galleries on Merseyside, Liverpool, Eng.; National Park Service, Colonial National Historical Park, Jamestown, Va.; North Carolina Division of Archives and History, Raleigh, N. C.; Old Sturbridge Village, Sturbridge, Mass.; Peabody and Essex Museum, Salem, Mass.; Pennsbury Manor, Morrisville, Pa.; Redwood Library and Athenaeum, Newport, R. I.; Rhode Island Historical Society, Providence, R. I.; Science Museum, London, Eng.; Sheffield City Library and Archives, Sheffield, Eng.; Society for the Preservation of New England Antiquities, Boston, Mass.; Sotheby's, London, Eng.; Stanley-Whitman House, Farmington, Conn.; Tate Gallery, London, Eng.; Upper Canada Village, Morrisburg, Ont., Can.; Victoria and Albert Museum, London, Eng.; Virginia Department of Historic Resources, Richmond, Va.; Virginia Historical Society, Richmond, Va.; and Virginia State Library and Archives, Richmond, Va. Many other museums and libraries made their collections available to us for study and aided us in our research. The Department of Materials Science and Engineering, Lehigh University, Bethlehem, Pa., is undertaking scientific analysis of a sample group of early edge tools in conjunction with our research.

Hank Allen, Roy Arnold, Alan G. Bates, William Bradshaw Beverley, Frank W. Blake, Daniel J. Comerford III, Theodore R. Crom, Richard Daly and Laurie Evans-Daly, Harry Derstler, Barry and Carol Eisenberg, William H. Guthman, Jim Hill, Edward Ingraham, Trip Kahn, Paul B. Kebabian, Gene Kijowski, Malcolm G. MacGregor, Duncan McNab, Hazel and Joseph Marcus, Ronald W. Pearson, D.O., Roger B. Phillips, Martyl and Emil Pollak, Jane and Mark Rees, Sidney F. Sabin, Roger K. Smith, Philip Walker, Byron B. Wenger, Hampton Williams, and Donald and Anne Wing all lent objects or images for the book or exhibit. Many other collectors, dealers, and scholars of historical technology let us examine their collections, shared their knowledge with us, fed us dinner, and offered us accommodations during our travels. Of special assistance were Frank White and DeWitt Bailey. Joseph Hutchins and Trip Kahn had the courage to accompany Jay on research and loan collection trips. Kathy Roletter provided constant encouragement and support.

Finally, we must thank the consultants who helped shape our early ideas and aspirations into concrete concepts: John Brewer, Marley Brown, Cary Carson, Charles Hummel, Melvin Kranzberg, Benjamin Lawless, Melora McDermott-Lewis, and Ralph Appelbaum Associates, Inc. Those who read the manuscript and pointed out our fallacies of fact or argument—Barbara Carson, Harold B. Gill, Charles Hummel, Paul Kebabian, Philip Walker, Emil Pollak, and Donald and Anne Wing—also have our gratitude for their knowledgeable help. Many of their suggestions are reflected here, but we can be stubborn, and any mistakes or misconceptions that remain are ours alone.

This book is going to press in mid-1993. Many others will assist us before the exhibit opens. We regret that we cannot include them here and offer our apologies to those others who, because of our faulty memories, we have failed to mention. They too have our sincerest appreciation.

Introduction

Tools have stories to tell. Agricultural implements, kitchen utensils, craft tools, and personal gadgets were among the most common and important possessions of early Americans. When Europeans first settled America, tools were vital to survival. Only by taking an ax or hammer or hoe in hand could colonists clear land, build shelter, and grow food. Over the next two centuries, tools remained essential for running a household and earning a living, and they were the means by which artisans transformed wood, metal, leather, clay, and fibers into a myriad of products that both sustained life and made it more comfortable. By looking closely at the ways tools functioned and how people used them, we can learn about the everyday tasks of early Americans and understand more fully the jobs they accomplished and the things they made.

Tools that once were the common stuff of everyday life are tools of a different sort to us. They no longer are the implements we use routinely to sustain ourselves; instead, they are tools we can use to understand the past. They are inanimate objects, however, and just as their original owners had to learn to use them productively, we have to ask the right questions of them to unlock their secrets.

Woodworking tools offer special opportunities for exploring early American life. At the time of settlement, most of the eastern seaboard was a land of wood, and the earliest colonists found themselves in the midst of a seemingly endless supply of timber. They cleared it for planting, building sites, and roads, and they harvested it for fuel and to construct fences, furniture, houses, vehicles, and ships. Throughout the eighteenth and early nineteenth centuries, Americans continued to transform wood into a vast array of products. Of all manufacturing and craft implements, woodworking tools were the most commonly owned. They survive in far greater numbers than tools used in other manufacturing trades, and they

are the types most frequently found at archaeological sites. Documents contain a relative abundance of information about them. Just as important, the makers of many woodworking tools stamped them with their names, and sets of carpentry and joinery implements have survived with histories of ownership and use. Often we can determine who made the tools and when, and by looking at the trades and products of their owners, we can discover how they were used.

What are the questions we ask of these tools? If we inquire who made them and why, we learn that most were the products of highly skilled, professional toolmakers. Many were manufactured in England, where the toolmaking trades were highly developed. English makers produced huge quantities of tools and looked to America as an important market for their wares. Other tools were made in America by woodworkers, local blacksmiths, and a few commercial toolmakers. If we ask how these tools came into the hands of craftsmen, we discover that the marketing of imported tools was sophisticated and they were readily available to most Americans. In contrast, American toolmakers served primarily local markets. Availability of new tools, however, was only one factor among many that influenced how artisans acquired their implements.

What of the quality of these tools? How could such wonderful buildings, chairs, chests-of-drawers, wagons, and boats be made with the "crude implements" of two centuries ago? Close study reveals that these devices are more complex than frequently has been assumed, and their apparent simplicity is often the result, not of naïveté, but of elegant refinement. A staggering variety of tool types, many highly specialized, allowed skilled users to create their products with efficiency and accuracy. We also find that tools influenced the daily routines of their users, the organization of their trades, and the qualities and characteristics of the things they made.

Since the early 1900s, collectors, craftspeople, and curators have studied old tools. For the most part, they have concentrated on nineteenth-century implements that survive in much larger quantities and are more fully documented. Because of their rarity, eighteenth-century tools have been given much less attention. For some questions, answers are well documented by historical records, surviving products, and the tools themselves. For others, we have much to learn, and the search for eighteenth-century tools and information about them is only just beginning.

This study concerns woodworking tools with an emphasis upon their ownership and use in eighteenth-century Virginia, but its conclusions are more universal. American artisans working in other trades such as blacksmithing, silversmithing, and leather and textile manufacturing used tools of equal quality and capabilities, and the influence of their tools was just as far-reaching. But those are stories for others to contemplate.

English and American Toolmaking

By the beginning of the seventeenth century, English craftsmen had been making products of wood for thousands of years and their tools reflected centuries of experimentation and refinement. During the next two hundred years, markets for wooden products expanded at home and in colonies abroad. The number of woodworkers grew accordingly and more tools were needed to outfit them. At the same time, the increasing complexity of many products led artisans to seek new and improved tools. Encouraged by larger markets, easier access to high-quality steel and other toolmaking materials, and an economic climate that favored domestic manufacturing, the English tool industry grew rapidly in both size and sophistication. The tools available to woodworkers improved dramatically during the period.

Saws and edge tools such as augers, chisels, and plane blades had long been made by specialist smiths equipped with the necessary skills and implements. As the tool industry expanded, the numbers of these specialists increased and new toolmaking trades emerged. Some began commercial production of implements that traditionally had been homemade, like bitstocks and the wooden bodies of planes. Thomas Granford and Robert Hemings, the first documented English specialist planemakers, were working in London by about 1690.[1] Others began large-scale production of tools often formerly made by local smiths, such as axes and hammers.

The English tool industry was well established and efficiently organized by the mid-eighteenth century. It produced an immense array of excellent tools that were readily available to woodworkers in both Britain and her colonies. Although planemakers and edge tool makers continued to work throughout the country, the manufacture of tools was largely centered in towns and regions that had skilled

1. European woodworking tools recovered from seventeenth-century Virginia archaeological sites. Top: gouge, ax, and compasses from Martin's Hundred near Williamsburg, ca. 1620–1640. The ax head is 6 5/8" long. 7787-50HA; 7875-50BA; 7788-50HA. Bottom: mortise chisel, tongue-plane iron, saw wrest, drill bit, wedge, and hammer head from Flowerdew Hundred, a plantation on the James River about twenty-five miles west of Williamsburg, 1618–1730. PG3/25; 44PG65/193L1-6; 44PG66/508B1-92; 44PG65/190/53-22; 44PG65/ 193N3D-4; 44PG64/2C/SWQ. Flowerdew objects courtesy of the Flowerdew Hundred Foundation.

2. Thomas Granford advertised in 1703 that he marked his planes with his full name. This molding plane is the only one known with this mark. OL: 10 5/16". Courtesy of the Paul B. Kebabian Collection.

labor, access to raw materials, and advantages such as large markets, good transportation, or waterpower for operating forges, grinding wheels, and other heavy machinery. London, Birmingham, Sheffield, and southwest Lancashire emerged as the primary centers, each specializing in one or more types of tools.

London was a traditional center of hand tool production and supply. Its craftsmen constituted a large market for tools, and its busy port made it a natural focus of national and international trade in implements of all types. Local demand for carpentry and joinery tools was probably increased by the Great Fire of 1666 and the building activity that followed. That stimulus, combined with the growing taste for elaborate furniture, architectural interiors, and other woodwork in the late seventeenth century, may have done much to encourage the growth of the city's toolmaking trades.[2]

Saws and planes seem to have been the most important woodworking tools produced in London during the eighteenth century. The ongoing manufacture of saws may have been largely the result of tradition. Planemakers found the style-setting capital city to be an advantageous location since many of their products were designed to cut fashionable moldings. In addition, many other tools became increasingly available

3. Toolmaking centers in eighteenth-century England.

from provincial toolmaking centers. As transportation throughout England improved, London tool retailers relied upon products from Birmingham, Sheffield, and Lancashire.[3] Shunned initially because of their supposed inferiority, the reasonable cost and improving quality of provincial tools soon made them acceptable and possibly even preferred. One London observer noted in 1747 that most edge tools, files, and hammers sold in the capital were "made in the Country."[4]

Birmingham area metalworkers supplied London, provincial England, Wales, Ireland, and the American colonies with a wide range of nails, locks, and other forged metalwares as early as the mid-seventeenth century. Birmingham's prominence in the hardware trades continued during the eighteenth century. Local artisans also became known for their production of guns and small metalwares, called "toys," such as buckles, buttons, personal accessories, and household utensils made of iron, steel, and brass.

The same skills and marketing networks that supported Birmingham's production of hardware and small metalwares also encour-

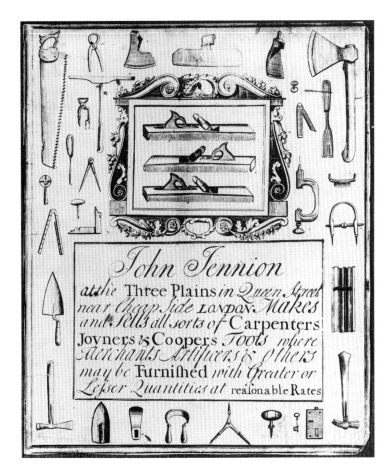

4. Trade card of London planemaker John Jennion, ca. 1740. Jennion apparently was also a tool merchant, offering implements he obtained from other makers as well as his own products. Heal Collection, 118.8, courtesy of the Trustees of the British Museum.

5. Eighteenth-century saw and edge tools made in Birmingham. Dovetail saw by Robert or William Dalaway; gouge, socket chisel (with new handle), and larger plane blade by Robert Moore; molding plane blade, probably by Aron Hildick (thought to be a Birmingham maker); mortise chisel by John Allen; and turning chisel by Sampson Freeth. Dovetail saw OL: 15". 1990-100; courtesy of the Framingham Historical and Natural History Society, Framingham, Mass.; 1984-184; courtesy of Martyl and Emil Pollak; courtesy of the Paul B. Kebabian Collection; 1990-236; 1992-199.

aged toolmaking. Early in the eighteenth century, Birmingham was an important producer of edge tools. Blades by Hildick (thought to be Birmingham) and Robert Moore (possibly father and son, 1721–1776) are found in early to mid-century London planes. Among the earliest documented English tools to survive are Birmingham chisels by John Allen (1767–1791), Samuel and Sampson Freeth (1767–1776), and Robert or William Dalaway (1746–1809); axes by Robert Moore and the Freeths; and saws by William Smith (1718–1750), the Dalaways, and Thomas Barnard (1777–1797). As the working dates of these makers indicate, Birmingham continued to produce edge tools and saws throughout the eighteenth century. After mid-

century, however, Sheffield increasingly dominated English edge tool and saw manufacture, and Birmingham toolmakers began to concentrate their efforts in other areas. They were the major suppliers of hammers, pincers, compasses, gimlets, bits, and other small metal tools. Birmingham makers also produced rules and planes. Compasses by Samuel Ault (1767–1781), gimlets by John Lightfoot (1765–1776, 1785–1809), rules by Thomas Onion (1767–1805), planes by Benjamin Frogatt (1760–1790), and a variety of tools made or sold by Benjamin Freeth (1767–1824) are among those most frequently found today.

Sheffield artisans had been known throughout England as producers of quality cutlery wares since at least the sixteenth century. By 1721, the region supported more than six thousand cutlers, edge tool makers, and other ironworkers.[5] Over the next fifty years, Sheffield's abundant natural resources of coal, waterpower, and sandstone for high-quality grindstones—combined with its large pool of skilled labor, increased steel production, and expanded access to markets through improved transportation—resulted in the dramatic growth of all its industries. By the late eighteenth century, Sheffield had become England's major producer of chisels, saws, axes, drawknives, and other cutting tools. Judging by the relative-

6. Birmingham tools. Folding rule by T. & G. Cox (ca. 1800); compasses by Sam Ault; timber scribe by T. Symond[s?], dated 1770; gimlet by John Lightfoot; molding plane by George Darbey (1750–1784). The gentleman's claw hammer, drawbore pin, saw wrest, and pincers, although unmarked, are attributed to Birmingham based on their designs. The hammer is ca. 1772; the drawbore pin, saw wrest, and pincers are late eighteenth or early nineteenth century. Hammer OL: 14 1/8". G1986-268, 49, gift of Frank M. Smith; 1990-121; 1992-80; W36-1593, Stephen C. Wolcott Collection; 1988-490; 1957-123, A2; 1991-159, 1; 1992-115; pincers courtesy of Trip Kahn—Rockhill Research.

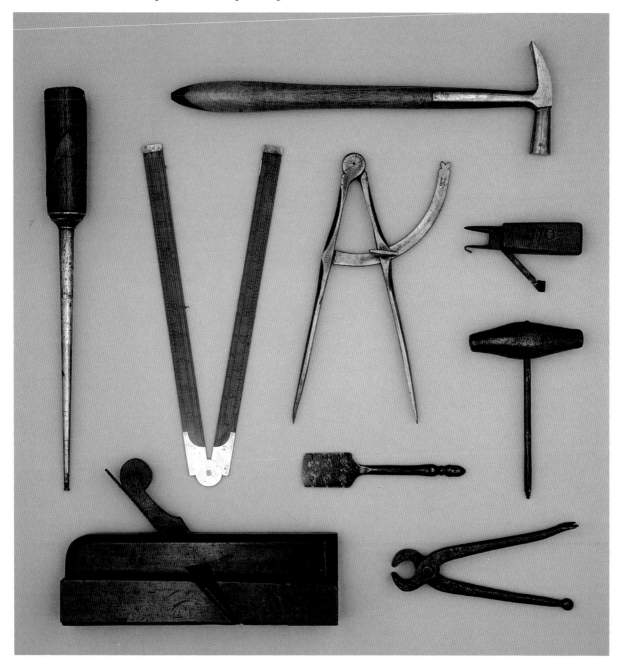

7. Edge tools by Philip Law of Sheffield. Top to bottom: carving chisel, mortise chisel, large paring chisel, gouge, plow plane blade, and jack plane blade. All late eighteenth to early nineteenth century. Large paring chisel OL: 13 7/8".
1989-409, 8; 1989-269; 1984-169; 1989-261; 1988-493, 1; 1957-123, A6.

ly large numbers of their products that survive, Sheffield toolmakers of this period like the Greens, Thomas and Samuel Newbould, Philip Law, James Cam, William Weldon, and John Kenyon were well known throughout England and America for their quality tools. All of these makers or their successors continued production well into the nineteenth century.

Toolmakers in southwest Lancashire were noted for producing carefully finished tools for clock- and watchmakers. Their pliers, vises, dividers, and files also were in demand by woodworkers who did finely detailed work. Thomas Hutton, a London watchmaker, asserted in 1773 that Lancashire tools were the best made in England, and many, particularly small files, were highly regarded throughout Europe.[6]

Most English toolmakers operated small shops in which only one or two journeymen and

8. Lancashire tools for watch and clock work were renowned for their high quality and fine finish. Riveting hammer, tail vise, and small anvil or beak iron. Hammer and beak iron ca. 1772; vise late eighteenth or early nineteenth century. None is marked. Hammer OL: 12 1/4".
1957-123, A4; 1982-182; 1957-123, A15.

Tools: Working Wood in Eighteenth-Century America

several apprentices were employed. During the early eighteenth century, most of these toolmakers probably marketed their own wares. Later, many Birmingham, Sheffield, and Lancashire toolmakers contracted their shops to supply specific products or services to large-scale tool manufacturers and wholesale merchants. Some of the small shops remained independent, purchasing their own materials and selling their products to merchant-manufacturers. Others, however, functioned as part of a system that became common in many English industries. Merchant-manufacturers supplied or "put-out" raw materials, tool components, and occasionally even toolmaking tools to their workers. Each shop then either manufactured a limited range of tools or undertook one or more specific processes required in the tools' manufacture such as casting, forging, assembling, or finishing. The merchant-manufacturer paid the shop by the piece for its work (a portion of that payment often consisting of another batch of materials), coordinated any other steps required in the overall production process, and marketed the finished tools.

This system had far-reaching effects on the production, quality, and cost of English hand tools. Since the nature of each shop's production was limited, both the fabrication and the quality of its wares could be highly refined. Skilled labor was plentiful, and competition kept production costs low. The production of tools to patterns or specifications supplied by merchant-manufacturers and the use of jigs to speed production encouraged standardization of designs and quality. Toward the end of the century, manufacturers such as Peter Stubs, a well-known Lancashire toolmaker, combined the putting-out system with centralized production, further improving quality control. Competition among toolmakers also led to improvements in tools. Makers who developed better quality or more useful tools increased their sales, encouraging innovations in materi-

9. Many English toolmakers worked in small shops located in or near their homes. The working and living conditions of this Birmingham nailmaker probably differed little from that of many metalworkers who made tools under the "putting out" system. Ink and wash drawing, ca. 1800, England, by J. Barber (1758–1811). Reproduced by permission of Birmingham City Museums and Art Gallery, Birmingham, Eng.

als and designs throughout the industry. All of these factors promoted the large-scale manufacture of high-quality, reasonably priced tools.

British colonial policy encouraged Americans to purchase goods from the mother country, and English manufacturers, including toolmakers, cultivated the colonies as a major market for their products. Shipping charges during the eighteenth century were based upon volume rather than weight, so tightly packed barrels and bales of hand tools could be transported from England to America inexpensively. Large quantities of English tools and other small wares flowed into the colonies and were readily available to most American consumers.

The availability of English tools undoubtedly limited the demand for locally made implements, but a number of other circumstances also discouraged the growth of an American tool industry. British regulations prohibiting colonial manufactures intended for export had only a minor impact on American toolmaking, but other practical considerations hampered large-scale, and therefore efficient and economical, production. America did not have abundant supplies of inexpensive skilled labor. Large quantities of raw materials such as steel were not available. With the exception of movement by water, transportation was difficult and expensive and American distribution systems tended to be narrowly focused to serve relatively small geographical regions. As a result, American makers' markets were primarily local ones, which were limited and unable to support highly specialized toolmakers. These factors created a situation that offered little incentive to invest precious capital in commercial tool manufacture.

American toolmakers also had to contend with the excellent reputation of English tools. Early American woodworkers were familiar with the style and performance of those tools, and many believed them to be the best available. American artisans who had access to imported tools evidently saw little need to turn to local manufacturers whose products might be inferior.

Virginia Council President James Blair noted the overall effect of these adverse conditions in 1768. He contended that the colonists did "not make a saw, auger, gimlett, file, or nails, iron [or] steel; and most tools in the Country are imported from Britain."[7] Americans did rely heavily on English tools, but Blair's assessment was not entirely correct.

Individual woodworkers in Virginia and throughout America followed age-old craft traditions and routinely made some types of tools. Many, such as wooden squares, bevels, and gauges, were easy to make. Large clamps and the array of jigs used in many trades were not available commercially. Artisans developed wooden or paper patterns for their products. Most tradesmen also made their own workbenches, vises, sawhorses, lathes, tool chests, and workshop fittings such as tool racks. They routinely fashioned the wooden portions of many tools whose blades were imported—handles and helves for edge tools, frames for saws, and, until late in the century, when commercial-

10. Samuel Wing, a cabinetmaker, chairmaker, and boatbuilder working in Sandwich, Massachusetts, from about 1795 to 1815, used these homemade pine patterns to fashion knife box ends and Windsor chair seats and crest rails. Crest rail pattern OL: 27". Courtesy of Old Sturbridge Village, Sturbridge, Mass., 86.32.5SW; 86.32.4SW; 86.32.3SW.

Tools: Working Wood in Eighteenth-Century America

ly manufactured examples began to supplant them, braces and bench planes. Woodworkers also modified tools to suit special needs. Molding planes were reshaped, worn files were converted to chisels and screwdrivers, and broken saw blades were cut up and made into scrapers.

It is likely that, upon occasion, craftsmen who were not commercial toolmakers made tools for sale. In 1789, William Allason, a Falmouth, Virginia, storekeeper, docked the pay of his employee, joiner Jacob Haines, for "Sundry Planes made for yourself while in my service." To make matters worse, Haines sold some of them for his own profit on the side, an act that Allason failed to appreciate.[8]

Local blacksmiths frequently repaired damaged tools, produced some simpler edge tools, and occasionally made special or unusual tools. Their account books contain numerous entries for making and resteeling axes, mending

11. Clamps made by Samuel Wing. Screw clamp jaws 18 1/2" long. Courtesy of Old Sturbridge Village, Sturbridge, Mass., 86.7.5SW; 86.7.9SW.

12. Virginia homemade tools. The pair of compasses and adjustable bevel were found in a wall of Woodlawn, a house in Goochland County. They probably were left there when the house was constructed during the fourth quarter of the eighteenth century. The small square was found in a Williamsburg dwelling. Bevel OL: 15 3/8". G1985-203 and G1985-202, gift of Mr. and Mrs. Thomas C. Kennedy; G1933-491, gift of Miss Lottie Garrett.

English and American Toolmaking

13. Members of the Dominy family of East Hampton, Long Island, worked in this shop from about 1760 to 1840. Like most American woodworkers, they made their own workbenches, tool storage shelves and racks, and lathes. Courtesy of Winterthur Museum, Winterthur, Del.

Tools: Working Wood in Eighteenth-Century America

14. Modified tools and make-dos. A square, dated 1809, made from a Kenyon hand-saw blade by Samuel Wing of Sandwich, Massachusetts; a chisel by the Sheffield maker Malin Gillot (1774–1797) reforged into a gouge; a pair of blacksmith's tongs converted to a nail puller; a pair of compasses by Freeth (probably Benjamin) re-shaped to form calipers for inside and outside measurements; and a saw blade made into a scraper. Square blade OL: 22 3/8". Square, nail puller, and scraper courtesy of Old Sturbridge Village, Sturbridge, Mass., Samuel Wing Collection, 86.16.1SW; 86.25.2SW; 86.26.1SW; gouge courtesy of Edward Ingraham; calipers courtesy of Trip Kahn—Rockhill Research.

15. Screwdrivers made from a sword blade and a file. The blade is probably from an early to mid-eighteenth-century colichemarde or small sword; the file is by Henry Smith of Sheffield (1774–1825). Sword screwdriver OL: 12 1/4". 1992-181; 1987-743.

English and American Toolmaking

saws, and altering tools. In the South, many of these smiths were slaves. Virginia Governor Francis Fauquier stated in 1767 that "every Gentleman of much property in Land and Negroes, have some of their own Negroes bred up in the Trade of black smiths, and make Axes, Hoes, plough shares, and such kind of coarse Work for the Use of their Plantations."[9]

Even under the best of circumstances, it could take two to three months to obtain a tool specially ordered from England. If the tool was not readily available from British suppliers, the delay could be longer. To make matters worse, instructions and designs sent to England were subject to misinterpretation, as gentleman plant-er Raleigh Downman of northern Virginia discovered. In July 1770, he asked his London agents Messrs. Clay and Midgley to send him, among other things, "one large & best bramble Alias Gum tooth Cross Cutt Saw," and "One best Carpenters Broad Ax." Downman was "greatly disappointed" with the two items when they finally arrived one year later. Instead of a house carpenter's broad ax, his agents had sent him a ship carpenter's. As for the crosscut saw, Downman complained that, in spite of his careful description of what he wanted, Clay and Midgley sent him "what is generally call'd a Tenant Saw" by mistake. "It cuts but one way and therefore does not answer my purpose."[10]

16. Blacksmith-made tools. Left to right: compasses, drawknife, tapered reamer, drill bit, scorp (curved drawknife), splitting wedge, and froe (also a splitting tool). The drawknife and tapered reamer were made from used files, a good source of high-quality steel. Assigning dates to blacksmith-made tools is difficult; these probably are 1775–1850. Drawknife OL: 14". 1950-204; W36-2511, Stephen C. Wolcott Collection; courtesy of the Paul B. Kebabian Collection; courtesy of Old Sturbridge Village, Sturbridge, Mass., Samuel Wing Collection, 86.19.11SW; W36-423 and W36-555, Stephen C. Wolcott Collection; Fred Bair Collection.

Tools: Working Wood in Eighteenth-Century America

17. Pennsylvania hewing axes by (left) Philip His, Lancaster County, and (right) "FK" (possibly Frederick Kerfen, Lancaster County); side (hewing) hatchet by MS (probably Michael Sower, Lancaster County); and tapered reamer by I. Gilbert (location unknown). All are late eighteenth or early nineteenth century. Their designs are based on those of Germanic tools. Reamer OL: 22 1/2". Left ax and reamer courtesy of the collection of Byron B. Wenger; right ax and hatchet from a private collection.

When confronted with similar problems, many American woodworkers undoubtedly chose to find a competent local smith to make the desired tool or modify a readily available imported one. In remote areas where local store-keepers stocked only the most basic tools, woodworkers turned to local blacksmiths to supply additional implements. Similarly, when cash was scarce, craftsmen could barter with local smiths for the tools they needed. In some regions, these local makers produced sizable quantities of tools. Pennsylvania German smiths made large numbers of heavy edge tools in the Continental styles preferred by their customers.

Some tools were manufactured commercially in Virginia and throughout the colonies. Settlers in the northern colonies quickly established towns whose markets and cash-based economy encouraged local manufacture of many needed goods. While still depending heavily on English imports, tool manufacturing developed more rapidly in these colonies than elsewhere. In southeastern New England, woodworkers began to specialize in the production of planes.

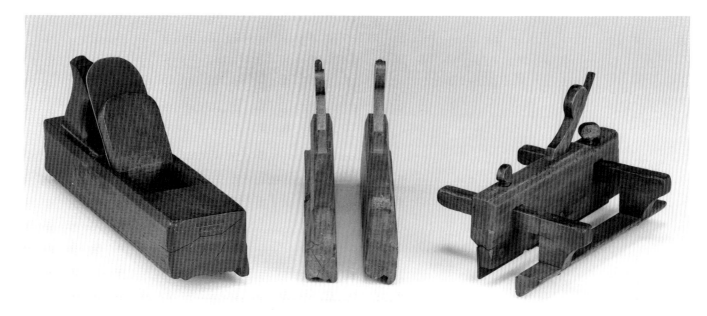

18. Planes by Francis Nicholson of Wrentham, Massachusetts. Left to right: a cornice plane, a pair of planes for forming the quadrant-shaped joints between table tops and their leaves, and a plow. Courtesy of the Paul B. Kebabian Collection; Donald and Anne Wing; and Martyl and Emil Pollak.

Francis Nicholson, the earliest known American specialist planemaker, was working in Wrentham, Massachusetts, by 1728. A number of other woodworkers in southeastern Massachusetts and Rhode Island were making substantial numbers of planes by the 1770s. Professional planemakers also began working outside New England before the Revolution. Several of the best documented were located in Philadelphia. Samuel Caruthers advertised his planes in the *Pennsylvania Chronicle* in the 1760s, and Thomas Napier, a planemaker from Edinburgh, Scotland, set up business in the city in 1774.[11] Like their English counterparts, most of these planemakers made only the wooden parts of their tools and many fitted them with blades made in Birmingham or Sheffield.

Other commercial makers made edge tools. Samuel Daniel of Middlesex County, Virginia, advertised in the *Virginia Gazette* in 1775 that "on

19. Philadelphia-made planes. A cornice plane by Samuel Caruthers (1767–d. 1780); a molding plane by Caruthers's apprentice Benjamin Armitage, Jr. (1760–1772); and two rounding planes (planes with their bottoms curved side-to-side) by Thomas Napier (1774–d. 1812). Courtesy of Martyl and Emil Pollak; 1989-196, 1 and 2.

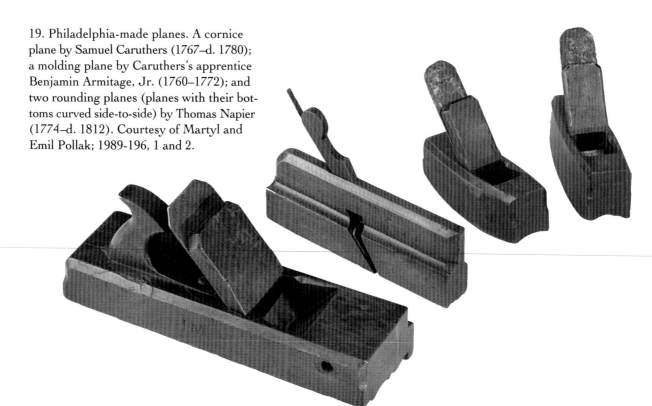

proper encouragement" he would supply his county "and a large number more, with all kinds of PLANTERS AND CARPENTERS TOOLS, no ways inferiour to those imported."[12] Some of these toolmakers were English immigrants. In 1734, "English smith" Isaac Harrow established a plating and blade mill in Trenton, New Jersey, and advertised in a Philadelphia newspaper that he made axes, saws, and various other carpenters' and coopers' tools.[13] Forty years later, William Ashburn, a "cutler from London," opened a shop near the Capitol in Williamsburg where he ground and repaired "all Sorts of Edge Tools" and made cutlery.[14] Several New York City toolmakers like Thomas Yates from Birmingham made "all sorts of small Steel and Iron Tools . . . such as Chizzels, Gouges, Drills, Scorpers, Gravers, Punchers, &c. &c."[15]

In 1731, Governor William Gooch of Virginia informed the Board of Trade in London that New England ironworks produced "Hoes, Axes, and other Utensils," at least some of which found their way into southern stores.[16] By the 1770s, James Hunter's forge on the Rappahannock River near Fredericksburg, Virginia, and Providence Forge in New Kent County turned out axes, hoes, and wedges as well as other iron wares.

Most commercial toolmaking efforts remained small until given a boost by the American Revolution. During the late 1760s and early 1770s, various nonimportation agreements forced Americans to find new sources of supply for tools. Supporting American manufactures was considered patriotic, and organized efforts were made to establish toolmaking enterprises in the colonies. In 1767, a group of New York entrepreneurs attempted to recruit Sheffield sawmakers to set up a manufactory.[17] During the war, local blacksmiths were called upon to supply the army with tools, and in 1779 Congress ordered the procurement of an extensive range of English tools to be sent to Ostende, Belgium, for shipment to America in the hope they could "serve as models" for American toolmakers.[18]

After the Revolution, the emphasis upon domestic manufactures continued. The ranks of New England planemakers swelled. Growing numbers of planemakers in New York, Philadelphia, southeastern Pennsylvania, and Baltimore began plying the trade. Sawmakers began production in New England and Philadelphia. New England and Pennsylvania forges turned out axes and other heavy edge tools. In the Shenandoah Valley of Virginia, members of the Kern family were active toolsmiths and planemakers during the late eighteenth and early nineteenth centuries.[19] As trade with Britain was reestablished and English tools once again began to be imported and used throughout America, some of these attempts to make tools quickly died. Plane- and heavy edge tool making had found good markets, however, and imported tools were supplemented by ever-increasing quantities of American-made tools.

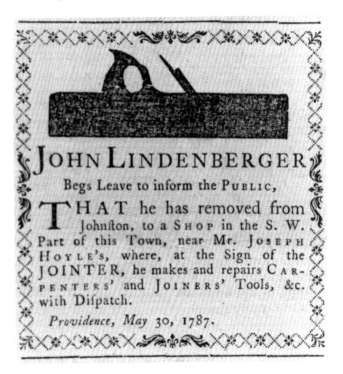

JOHN LINDENBERGER

Begs Leave to inform the PUBLIC,

THAT he has removed from Johnston, to a SHOP in the S. W. Part of this Town, near Mr. JOSEPH HOYLE's, where, at the Sign of the JOINTER, he makes and repairs CARPENTERS' and JOINERS' Tools, &c. with Difpatch.

Providence, May 30, 1787.

20. John Lindenberger (b. 1754–d. 1817), a planemaker of Providence, Rhode Island, ran this advertisement in the *U. S. Chronicle* (Providence, R. I.), June 14, 1787. Courtesy of the Rhode Island Historical Society, Providence, R. I.

Despite these successful efforts, tool manufacturing did not become a substantial industry in America until the second quarter of the nineteenth century. From that point on, American mechanical ingenuity, mechanized manufacturing capability, and access to wider markets through canals and railroads transformed a nation of tool importers into a nation of tool-makers that produced traditional and innovative tools inferior to none. Until then, American tools made "after the best Fashion" (i.e., English) and "equal in Goodness to any imported" continued to be overshadowed by good quality, affordable English tools in most American tool chests.[20]

21. Providence, Rhode Island, planemaker Joseph Fuller (b. 1746–d. 1822) wanted no one to mistake this plane for an imported tool. Courtesy of Martyl and Emil Pollak.

Tools: Working Wood in Eighteenth-Century America

Tools for Sale

One important factor in the success of the English tool industry was the sophisticated marketing system by which its wares were distributed. Wholesalers in London, Bristol, and other commercial centers distributed London, Birmingham, Lancashire, and Sheffield products to retailers throughout Britain. Many British tool manufacturers and merchants also depended upon overseas sales. London, Bristol, Liverpool, Whitehaven, and Glasgow thrived on international trade, and large quantities of all types of British manufactured goods, including tools, passed through these ports bound for the Continent, Africa, the West Indies, and America.

English toolmakers and tool merchants employed surprisingly modern techniques to sell their wares. To build "brand name" recognition, many makers stamped their names on the tools they made or bought from subcontractors. Makers who operated retail shops often specialized in the production of one type of tool and bought other types to increase the range of wares they offered. Traveling salesmen, or "outriders," representing toolmakers visited prospective customers to show them samples, encourage orders, and collect payments. Toolmakers and merchants handed out illustrated trade cards bearing their names and lists of their wares. Newspaper advertisements announced the availability, quality, and variety of tools for sale. Appealing window displays attracted the casual passerby. City directories listed toolmakers and dealers by name, trade, and location to inform prospective buyers from afar.

Toolmakers produced some of the earliest known English illustrated catalogs. They included engravings of tools and indicated the range of sizes and qualities available. John Wyke, a Lancashire watch and clock tool manufacturer, issued the first such catalog in the late 1750s.[21] It contained only the goods sold by Wyke's firm. Later catalogs of Birmingham and

Sheffield wares could be used by any manufacturer or wholesaler with the addition of an appropriate price list.

English toolmakers produced not only a vast array of tool types, but offered them in a variety of designs, sizes, and qualities to suit the needs, tastes, and pocketbooks of their customers. Birmingham pliers could be had "black" (unpolished) or finished to a "bright" surface at a higher price. A woodworker buying a chisel could chose between an ordinary one or one that was "best." Retailers offered saws made of different quality steels at a range of prices.

22. Most professional planemakers stamped their products with their names. These London molding planes for forming quarter-rounds (ovolos) are by John Jennion or his widow, Anna (1732–1778), and George Mutter (1766–1799), this plane ca. 1795. The other names are those of owners. 1985-97; 1983-7.

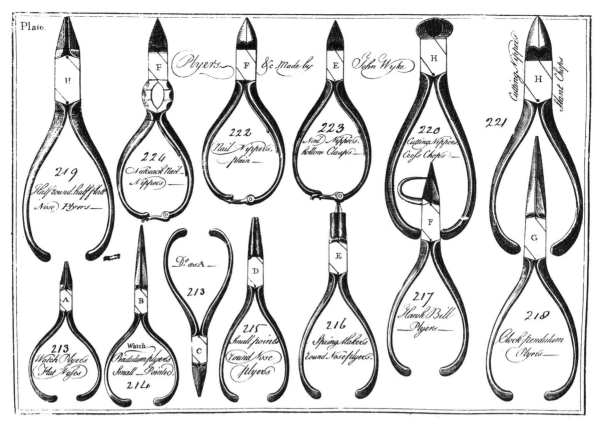

23. Pliers offered by Thomas Green of Liverpool in his catalog of ca. 1795. Green was a partner to and successor of John Wyke, and his catalog was printed from plates first used by Wyke. Courtesy of Ted Crom.

24. "Black [unpolished] Carpenters Hammers" illustrated in a catalog of Birmingham goods printed about 1800. Courtesy of the James Duncan Phillips Library, Peabody and Essex Museum, Salem, Mass.

Tools: Working Wood in Eighteenth-Century America

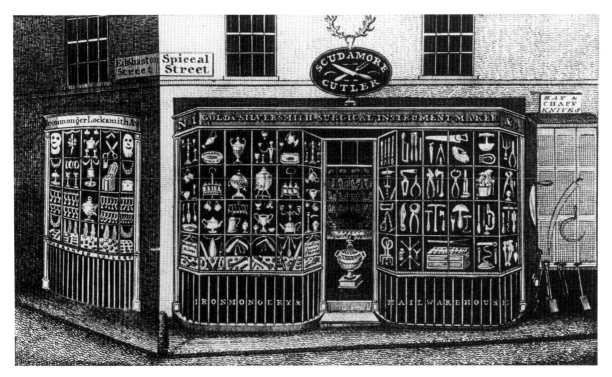

25. The shop of Thomas or Samuel Scudamore in Birmingham, late eighteenth or early nineteenth century, as illustrated on a trade card. Heal Collection, 52.94, courtesy of the Trustees of the British Museum.

Toolmakers and dealers sought to market their wares to general customers as well as to professionals. Catalogs offered special tools for "ladies" and "gentlemen." "Gentlemen's Tool Chests," the eighteenth-century equivalent of a modern handyman's tool set, were sold to homeowners, shopkeepers, and hobbyists. These kits were packaged in wooden chests available in several sizes. They contained anywhere from fifteen to seventy-five tools, plus an assortment of nails, screws, and other hardware. The smallest cost about one pound and the most elaborate about nine pounds at a time when a London journeyman cabinetmaker could expect to earn one to two pounds a week.[22]

Two gentlemen's tool chests sold by London ironmonger William Hewlett survive (fig. 26). One, purchased by an unknown customer on February 13, 1773, is constructed like a fashionable piece of London furniture and is covered with mahogany veneer. Hewlett probably obtained it from a London cabinetmaker.

Of the fifty-six tools originally sold with the chest, twenty-two remain. They are in nearly new condition. Some were London made; others were brought to London from Lancashire, Birmingham, and Sheffield. Many have mahogany, lignum vitae (an exotic hardwood), and brass parts instead of the usual beech and iron. The metal surfaces are finished bright, and several of the edge tools are stamped BEST—all features designed to appeal to an affluent customer. No tools remain with the second chest, which was sold by Hewlett at a slightly later date. The basic design of the two chests is similar and both have almost identical partitions and compartments. However, the second chest is made of oak and constructed using simpler joinery. It probably sold for about 15 percent less than the mahogany one. Apparently even gentlemen had pockets of varying depths.

From a practical standpoint, it was unnecessary to extend most British domestic marketing techniques to America. Orders placed by

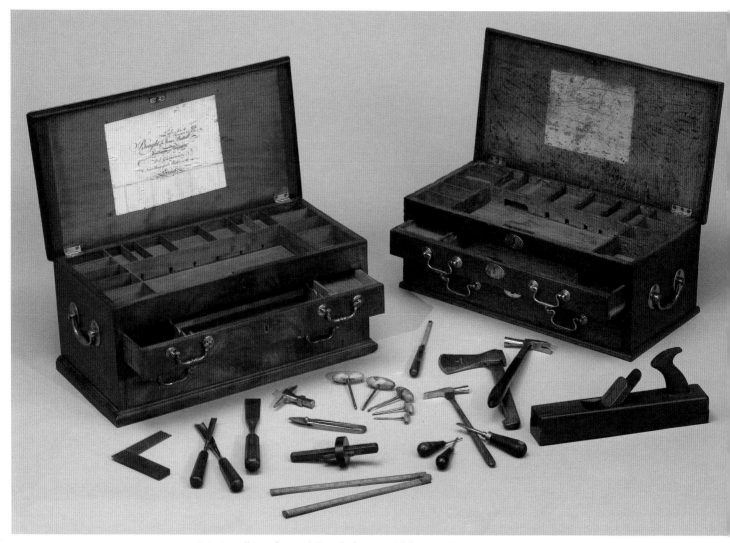

26. Two "Gentlemen's" tool chests sold by London ironmonger William Hewlett. The chests are about two feet wide. 1957-123; 1986-247.

Americans were usually quite general, specifying types and sizes but rarely mentioning other details or makers' names. These orders were sent to English agents, who gathered the tools required and shipped them to their customers. While English merchants and retailers may have found catalogs, directories, and trade cards useful in making their purchases and attracting customers, it would have served little purpose to distribute these publications in America. Once tools arrived, however, American retailers often advertised their availability in newspapers and no doubt displayed them in their shop windows.

American toolmakers also found little use for sophisticated marketing techniques since wide distribution of their wares usually was impractical. Nevertheless, many followed English practice and marked their products with their names, frequently including their locations as well. Urban toolmakers advertised in local newspapers, often including extensive lists of the items offered for sale.

Tools: Working Wood in Eighteenth-Century America

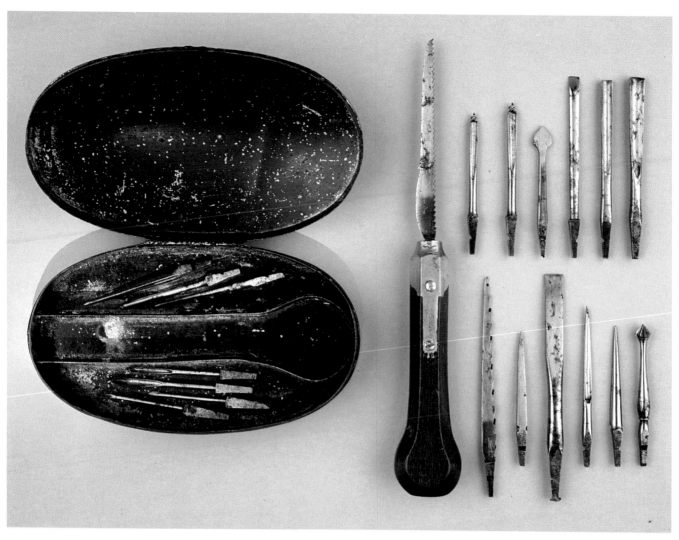

27. Birmingham toolmakers produced pocket tool kits like this one consisting of a handle with interchangeable blades sold by Freeth (probably Benjamin), and "snap joint" tools with folding blades ranging from corkscrews to hoof picks. Both are probably early nineteenth century. Handle with saw OL: 10 5/8"; snap-joint tool as shown OL: 4 3/4". 1991-459, acquired through the generosity of Sharon and James W. Swinehart; 1987-30.

Tools for Sale

28. Williamsburg cabinetmaker Anthony Hay and builder Christopher Ford, Jr., imported tools for resale to fellow artisans. *Virginia Gazette* (Williamsburg), March 21, 1755.

Throughout the New England and Middle Atlantic colonies, retail establishments were the most important sources for imported tools during the eighteenth century. Many stores carried tools among their general merchandise. Other retailers, including toolmakers who supplemented their own products with a selection of imported tools, were more specialized. Stores became the primary suppliers of tools in the South as well, but tool marketing evolved in a fashion distinct to that region's economy. The economy of the southern colonies was based almost entirely on the production and export of staple cash crops such as tobacco and rice. In return, colonists received credit with which they could buy British goods. This cash crop economy, coupled with the relatively slow development of towns and sizable local markets,

29. Levi Little (b. 1770–d. 1802) was a planemaker working in Boston, Massachusetts, who also imported English planes for resale. Before Little sold this plane made by Birmingham maker John Cox, Sr. (1770–ca. 1812), he stamped his own name over Cox's. Courtesy of Donald and Anne Wing.

30. This London molding plane by George Mutter (1766–1799) was retailed by the Philadelphia ironmongers T. Poultney & Sons, probably before 1798. Ironmongers sold the kinds of goods found in hardware stores today and often carried a wide variety of imported tools. Courtesy of Alan G. Bates.

31. The economy of the Chesapeake region of Virginia, Maryland, and North Carolina was dominated by the tobacco trade. Many of the coopers who made the hogsheads for shipping tobacco were slaves. This wharf scene is from the 1751 map of Virginia by Joshua Fry, professor of mathematics at the College of William and Mary, and Peter Jefferson, the father of Thomas. 1968-11.

encouraged southerners to import the vast majority of their small manufactured goods from England.

Woodworking and agricultural tools figured prominently in the supplies sent to Virginia's earliest settlers. Lists of provisions contained large quantities of axes for clearing the land, carpentry tools for building, and coopering tools for making staves and barrels, including the hogsheads in which tobacco was shipped to England.[23] Despite these tool imports, supplies remained limited. Tools were considered so valuable during the colony's first years that the government passed laws imposing strict punishments for those who lost, abused, or traded them without authorization.[24] As late as 1622, the Virginia Company spelled out in a promotional broadside the kinds and numbers of tools that settlers needed to bring for rudimentary household and farm construction and maintenance.[25]

The documentary record regarding woodworking tools in Virginia is sparse from the 1620s until the third quarter of the century, when surviving estate inventories begin to list the tools owned by planters and artisans. These inventories reveal that by the 1670s Virginians

THE INCONVENIENCIES

THAT HAVE HAPPENED TO SOME PERSONS WHICH HAVE TRANSPORTED THEMSELVES from *England* to *Virginia*, without provisions necessary to sustaine themselves, hath greatly hindred the Progresse of that noble *Plantation*: For prevention of the like disorders hereafter, that no man suffer, either through ignorance or misinformation; it is thought requisite to publish this short declaration: wherein is contained a particular of such necessaries, as either private families or single persons shall have cause to furnish themselves with, for their better support at their first landing in *Virginia*, whereby also greater numbers may receive in part, directions how to provide themselves.

32. Early settlers to Virginia were forewarned that they would need a basic kit of woodworking tools. Broadside issued by the Virginia Company, 1622. Courtesy of the John Carter Brown Library at Brown University.

apparently had ready access to a selection of carpentry and coopering tools either by importing them directly or by purchasing them from the supplies kept by large tobacco planters. Although there were professional carpenters, wheelwrights, and boatbuilders in Virginia, they were few in number and little is known about them. The tools that appear most commonly in late seventeenth-century records are general-purpose types.

Virginia's economy and society had begun to mature by the turn of the century. Population increased and towns were established. The demand for houses, mills, vehicles, and furniture, all built of wood, rose. The resulting growth in trades led to a need for more tools, which was met by greater importations of English implements. Most were obtained through wealthy planters who shipped their tobacco directly to agents in England on consignment and imported tools and other goods into Virginia with the credit earned.

As settlement spread west from the Virginia Tidewater, a new system of stores developed. In the 1730s, Scottish merchants sent agents, called "factors," to Virginia to purchase tobacco locally and ship it to Glasgow, which saved small planters the expense and risk of shipping it on consignment. As business grew, many factors found it profitable to set up permanent stores where they purchased the tobacco and sold a wide variety of goods, often on credit. In addition to an impressive array of foodstuffs, fabrics, clothing accessories, and housewares, these stores carried hardware and tools. The Scots were so successful that many English merchants followed suit. Some opened stores of their own, while others went into the wholesale business, supplying the vast quantities of goods required by retail stores. By the 1760s these stores became the principal source of imported tools for many Virginians.

Most rural Virginia storekeepers stocked a basic assortment of imported tools, and local woodworkers could obtain hammers, saws, chisels, planes, and other common tools through them. Some urban stores, such as John Greenhow's in Williamsburg, specialized in more complete selections of trade tools. In 1767, Greenhow advertised "tools and materials for all kinds of tradesmen."[26] Savvy merchants kept abreast of the latest tool developments and knew the best sources from which to obtain the best English implements at the lowest cost. Upon occasion, they even specified the makers of the tools they ordered.

Most American craftsmen lived within reach of a toolmaker or store that offered tools for sale. Individual circumstances, however, could limit an artisan's access to the tools he needed and wanted, and the ways in which woodworkers acquired their implements varied. Wealth, family, status—whether master or employee, freeman or slave—training and skills, local traditions, and personal preferences all affected choices artisans could make and the tools they obtained.

Many young woodworkers acquired their first tools during their apprenticeships. As they

To be SOLD at JOHN GREENHOW's store, Williamsburg,

CLOVER, lucern, and rye grass seed, camomile flowers, bark, camphor, vials, gallipots, sundry fresh drugs, sago, mixed sweetmeats, tamarinds, mustard, borax, spelter, emery, polishing powders, oil, stone slips, all sorts of spices, paints, oils, camel hair pencils, Indian ink, ringworm earth, harness buckels, brasses, and bits, desk furniture, brass nails, tea chest furniture and canisters complete, surveyors instruments complete or separate, chapes and tongs for silver buckles, pliers, seine cork and lead, lancets, tooth drawers, nippers, sliding tongs, pin vices, hand and bench vices, large and small cock gaffs, necklaces, crystals, main and pendulum springs, hour and minute hands, magnifiers, green, blue, and crystal convex and concave spectacles, glaziers diamonds, saddle trees of all sorts, curled hair, hank wire, vermine and beaver traps, files of all sorts, blacksmiths, saddlers, shoemakers, carpenters, joiners, silversmiths, and bricklayers tools, half gallon case bottles, wide mouth bottles, house bells, coffee mills, toys, fiddles, Roman strings, tin sheats, sifter and search bottoms, sithes and sickles, bird glasses, rum provers, wine by the gallon, cask, or pipe, locks and hinges of all sorts, most kinds of materials for building, window glass of all sizes, cart and chair wheel boxes, all sorts of cast iron, bar iron, chair traces, and many hundred other useful articles.

Run away, last December, from the said GREENHOW, an old Negro man named HARRY, by trade a cooper; he did belong to Col. Moseley of Princess Anne, and lived many years at Hampton, where he has children. It is supposed he is either about Hampton, Norfolk, or Newtown. He is a sly thief, few locks or doors will turn him, and is seldom long in a place before he puts his ingenuity in practice. Whoever conveys him to me shall be paid as the law directs. He is outlawed.

33. Williamsburg storekeeper John Greenhow offered "blacksmiths, saddlers, shoemakers, carpenters, joiners, silversmiths, and bricklayers tools." *Virginia Gazette* (Purdie and Dixon), April 11, 1766. Courtesy of the Virginia Historical Society, Richmond, Va.

Tools: Working Wood in Eighteenth-Century America

34. Many a young apprentice's first tool may have been a pocket knife, probably made in Sheffield. This basic implement continued to be useful for a variety of tasks throughout an artisan's working life. Top, knife by Joseph Binny, late eighteenth century; bottom, dated 1774, by John Barlow. Binny knife OL: 8 1/4". 1989-82 and 1989-72, Madison Grant Collection.

learned their trades at the side of an accomplished woodworker, making tool chests, squares, bevels, gauges, and tool handles provided both a way to begin assembling a tool kit and an opportunity to practice many woodworking skills. Apprenticeship agreements also often required that apprentices be given "freedom dues" upon completion of their training. Sometimes these freedom dues included tools. In most cases, tools received as freedom dues probably consisted of the commercially manufactured components of the basic tool kit of the trade. John Miller, an orphan apprenticed to a joiner in Lancaster County, Virginia, in 1725/6, was promised "necessary tools for his trade."[27] Twenty years later, John Garrow of York County, an apprentice carpenter, received "as many Carpenters tooles as will build a common Clabboard House."[28] In 1747, John Oen, another carpenter-to-be, was promised "one broad ax, one hand saw, one Augre [auger], one adze, one drawing knife, one Rule, one pare of Compasses, two Chisels."[29] The master's obligation to provide these tools was taken very seriously, and if he failed to do so, his apprentice could sue. Jonathan Parish found himself in this position following his master's unexpected death in

1726/7, and successfully sued the estate for "a set of Carpenters tools for course [coarse] work."[30]

While apprenticeship often equipped an artisan with basic tools, he frequently had to obtain additional implements elsewhere. He continued to make some types for himself. He might purchase others from local blacksmiths or fellow workmen. Many, however, were best acquired from commercial sources. In the North, he might have turned to local professional toolmakers for implements such as planes. In the South, commercially made usually meant imported.

If he had cash or could arrange credit, a woodworker could purchase new tools from the local store or order them from England. It is difficult to equate eighteenth-century prices with modern values; not only is there no simple formula for calculating inflation and other factors, but the circumstances of eighteenth-century life are so removed from those of today that priorities, and therefore the "value" of goods, were very different. A handsaw, one of the most expensive commonly owned woodworking tools, sold for five to six shillings in Virginia at mid-century. A common chisel sold for about one shilling, a molding plane for less than two. At the same time, an average Williamsburg journeyman earned about thirty pounds per year, or roughly two shillings per day. A master craftsman might clear as much as sixty to one hundred pounds annually.[31] To make these prices relevant to today, however, it must be realized that a chisel or handsaw allowed a woodworker to compete effectively with his fellows. Competition today usually requires ownership of power

tools, and their purchase can easily require a comparable investment.

Some artisans found it expedient to barter their services to earn credit for needed tools. In 1769, Reubin Berry, a cabinetmaker near Boyd's Hole, Virginia, made a "Show Box" for the store of John Glassford and Company and received credit that he used to purchase goods including tools.[32] Some slaves also obtained tools this way. Negro Jack did odd jobs in exchange for credit at his local store. Between July 1764 and November 1766, he received over two and one-half pounds' credit for making a pine table, constructing pigeonholes and bookshelves for a desk, moving some buildings and fences, and assisting with the storage of goods and rum. Jack used his credit to purchase some gimlets, a file for sharpening saws, a plane iron, and glue, among other things.[33]

Although most artisans bought individual tools as they needed them, affluent craftsmen could purchase entire kits outright. Orders sent to England for such sets can be found in the records of merchants. In 1768, storekeeper William Allason obtained a kit of nearly 230 joiner's tools from a fellow Virginia merchant for the wholesale price of £9.4.7.[34] Allason's tools do not survive, but a remarkable group of cabinetmaker's tools purchased as a set survives in England. On December 15, 1796, upholsterer and cabinetmaker Joseph Seaton of Chatham, Kent, bought his son Benjamin (d. 1834) about 200 cabinetmaker's tools from the London toolmakers and dealers Christopher Gabriel and Sons (figs. 36 and 37). Benjamin apparently added more than 60 commercial and homemade pieces and built a chest to hold them all. According to family tradition, Benjamin intended to come to America, bringing the tools with him. He never left England, however, and his virtually unused tools are preserved in the Guildhall Museum in Rochester, Kent.

Although Benjamin Seaton's tools never made it to America, the tool kits of many other artisans did. George William Cartwright II (1785–1867) emigrated from London to Ossining (Sing Sing), New York, in 1819.

35. An invoice for a set of English joiner's tools obtained by Falmouth, Virginia, storekeeper William Allason from storekeeper James Bowie of Port Royal, Virginia, May 31, 1768. David and William Allason Business Records, Business Records Collection, Archives and Records Division, Virginia State Library and Archives, Richmond, Va.

Tools: Working Wood in Eighteenth-Century America

Packed in a fitted chest, his tools included planes, saws, chisels, sharpening stones, marking and measuring tools, and implements for specialized tasks such as carving and veneering (fig. 38). Since many immigrant artisans brought tools of the most current fashion with them, their kits helped American artisans keep up with new tool developments in England. That may not have been the case with Cartwright's tools, however, since many had been made before he was born. He probably inherited or purchased them secondhand.

American artisans also had opportunities to obtain used tools more cheaply than new ones. In England, at least in urban areas, there apparently was a thriving trade in secondhand implements. Retiring workmen, local markets, and pawnshops were traditional sources, and by the end of the eighteenth century some commercial tool dealers advertised that they not only bought and sold secondhand tools but took old tools in exchange for new. Used tools probably were sold at markets and pawnshops in America as well, but most of the surviving

36. The Benjamin Seaton tool chest, 1797. It is 38" wide. Courtesy of the Guildhall Museum, Rochester, Kent, Eng.; photography by John Melville.

37. A selection of tools from the Seaton chest. Courtesy of the Guildhall Museum, Rochester, Kent, Eng.; photography by John Melville.

Tools: Working Wood in Eighteenth-Century America

38. Tools brought from London to New York by George William Cartwright II in 1819. The chest is 44 1/4" wide. G1986-268, gift of Frank M. Smith.

evidence concerns sales of tools by retiring craftsmen or of the estates of deceased woodworkers. When Williamsburg cabinetmaker Peter Scott decided to go to England in 1755, he advertised tools, materials, finished cabinet work, and "Two Negroes, bred to the Business of Cabinet-maker" for sale.[35] Executors sometimes disposed of the working tools of deceased artisans in order to pay off debts or provide financial support for dependents. John McCloud, a Petersburg cabinetmaker, specified in his 1796 will "that all my Shop Tools, Stock of Timber and materials for my business, with what furniture may be on hand in my Shop, may be Sold for the best price." He wanted the money to pay for his funeral expenses and debts, with the remainder going to his widow "for the purpose of Educating our children in the fear of the Lord."[36]

39. Pawnbrokers probably were ready sources of used tools. William Hogarth (b. 1697–d. 1764) depicted an English carpenter selling his saw and coat to buy gin. Detail from *Gin Lane*, line engraving, England, 1751. 1972-409, 94.

Tools for Sale

40. A selection of the Thomas and Warren Nixon tools. Most date to the
last quarter of the eighteenth century. The chest is 49 3/4" wide. Courtesy
of the Framingham Historical and Natural History Society, Framingham,
Mass.

Tools: Working Wood in Eighteenth-Century America

Bequests were another important source of used tools. Since young men often followed the trades of their fathers or uncles, it was common practice to bequeath tools to sons and nephews. In 1777, Charles Grim of Winchester left his son Charles a new house and lot, plus all his joinery tools. He expected Charles to "larne his Brother George Grim the art and mistery of the joiners trade."[37] As kits descended from generation to generation, old tools were used up and new ones were added to meet the needs of successive owners. One inherited kit, a rare survival, belonged to the Nixon family of Framingham, Massachusetts (fig. 40). Thomas Nixon (1762–1842) passed his carpenter's and joiner's tools along to his son Warren (1793–1872). According to local tradition, both men used the tools to construct their homes, the elder's completed in 1787 and the son's in 1836. The tools are now owned by the Framingham Historical and Natural History Society.

American newspaper advertisements and estate inventories indicate that some master woodworkers owned more tools than they could have used personally. John Clark of Richmond advertised in the *Virginia Gazette* in March 1776 that he intended to sell his lot and dwelling — which included rooms "in Order for a Cabinet-Maker's Shop, for which it has of late been used" — and "the Benches and Tools, which are sufficient to employ six Hands."[38] Masters of many shops provided their workmen with some tools, probably those too large, expensive, or highly specialized to be owned by individual journeymen.

Wealthy planters, among them George Washington and Thomas Jefferson, commonly furnished their slaves and employees with the tools they needed, often importing them directly through the English agents who handled the sale of their tobacco and grain. A Virginia historian wrote in 1724 that slaves "are taught to be sawyers, carpenters, smiths, coopers, etc."[39] Slaves also worked in the finer woodworking trades such as cabinetmaking and joinery. While they may have made some wooden tools or upon occasion purchased a tool locally, slaves usually had to be content with the tools their masters saw fit to supply.

American woodworkers obtained specific tools for a variety of reasons. Artisans selected some because they eased work. Others satisfied a personal whim. Sometimes craftsmen's purchases were motivated by the need to undertake new types of work requested by their customers. Some tools were bought because they were bargains; others came to the craftsman as gifts or bequests. The result was that American tool kits varied from elaborate to sparse, expensive to cheap.

Two American tool chests illustrate aspects of this variety. A kit housed in a type of chest found in New York and New England is owned by the Farmers' Museum in Cooperstown, New York (fig. 41). The chest itself probably was made about 1800. Many of the carpentry and joinery tools it contains are late eighteenth or early nineteenth century. Some were imported, some were locally made, and some were homemade. Both the chest and tools are straightforward, the kit of a working man who was concerned that his tools permit him to undertake the tasks at hand, but who saw little need for fancy frills. The second chest (fig. 42) was owned by the famous nineteenth-century New York cabinetmaker Duncan Phyfe (1768–1854). It is later than the Cooperstown chest, and although it contains many imported tools, its contents also suggest the growing availability of American commercially made implements. The Phyfe tools reflect a totally different attitude on the part of their owner. The chest is elegantly made in the English style. Phyfe bought and made for himself tools of the highest quality and finish, and they are arranged in the chest in neatly ordered drawers and racks. Much more than a simple container, Phyfe's tool chest was a consciously created masterpiece intended to advertise his skill and ornament his shop.

41. A chest of carpenter's and joiner's tools probably owned by an upstate New York craftsman. The chest is 41 1/8" wide. Courtesy of The Farmers' Museum, Inc., Cooperstown, N. Y., F-181.53.

Tools: Working Wood in Eighteenth-Century America

42. The tool chest of Duncan Phyfe (b. 1768–d. 1854). 39" wide.
Courtesy of an anonymous lender.

Tools and Work

Tools were among an artisan's most important possessions. Most early Americans who created products of wood did so to earn a living, and tools enabled them to practice their trades and to secure a roof over their heads, food to eat, clothes to wear, and the luxuries that made life more comfortable. English Common Law, which was in effect in the colonies, recognized the value of artisans' tools by stipulating that they were to be the last property seized for payment of debt. Even a craftsman's reputation among his fellows was influenced by the quality of his tools and the skill with which he used them.

There is ample evidence that most artisans valued their tools highly. Advertisements for runaway servants and slaves indicate that many took the tools of their trades with them in hopes of earning their livings as free men. Some arti-sans stamped or branded their names or initials on their tools to denote ownership. Woodworkers protected their tools in their shops by storing them in specially built racks. Carpenters and house joiners who carried their tools to job sites and artisans who worked alongside many others built fitted, lockable chests to safeguard their implements against damage, theft, and "borrowing." Such chests usually had plain, sturdy exteriors and strictly utilitarian interiors, although a few, like Duncan Phyfe's chest, were masterfully executed, bespeaking their makers' skill and pride.

Most English and American commercially made tools were straightforward and plain. Artisans who crafted tools for their own uses, however, sometimes employed exotic woods, bone, ivory, or brass. Occasionally craftsmen embellished homemade tools with extra decora-

43. Southeastern Pennsylvania woodworkers often branded their names into their tools. Front to back: jack plane by Samuel Caruthers, molding plane by William Martin (1773–1801), and jointer plane probably by John Butler (1791–1830), all of Philadelphia. Some of the brands may be those of second or third owners. Jack plane OL: 12". Courtesy of Martyl and Emil Pollak; 1982-134; 1992-25, acquired through the generosity of Mr. and Mrs. E. Charles Beyer.

Tools: Working Wood in Eighteenth-Century America

44. Interior of the lid of an English joiner's chest, ca. 1790.
OL: 44 1/2". Courtesy of Jane and Mark Rees.

tive touches or proudly carved or engraved them with their names and dates. These implements, as well as the more expensive commercially made tools, must have been especially valued possessions.

Artisans' attitudes toward their tools were shaped by their training. Some urban American woodworkers formed protective trade organizations during the late eighteenth century, but the guild system that governed trade practices in England was not transferred to the colonies. Although few restrictions regulated woodworking trades in America, English apprenticeship traditions did influence the ways by which young people were taught their trades. Apprenticeship

customs had their roots in the Middle Ages when the system served as a means of regulating the transmission of specialized trade skills and knowledge from one generation to the next, thereby safeguarding artisans' livelihoods. Such protection was unnecessary in America where skilled labor was in short supply, but since apprenticeship was an effective way to learn a trade, most American woodworkers were trained by working with an experienced artisan.

Training arrangements between family members often were informal; in other situations, however, apprenticeship agreements were legal contracts. In England, children generally were apprenticed at the age of fourteen for a

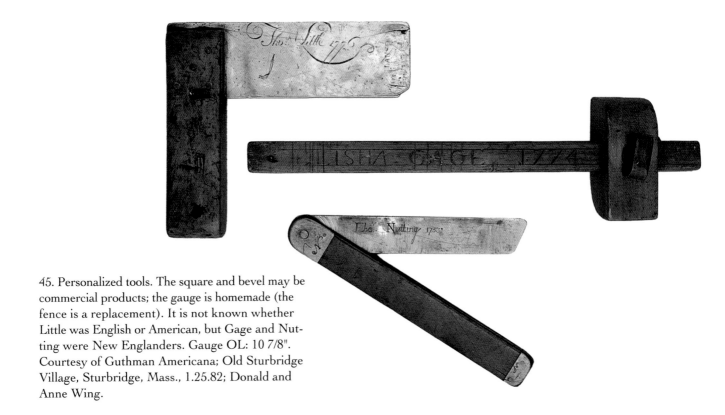

45. Personalized tools. The square and bevel may be commercial products; the gauge is homemade (the fence is a replacement). It is not known whether Little was English or American, but Gage and Nutting were New Englanders. Gauge OL: 10 7/8". Courtesy of Guthman Americana; Old Sturbridge Village, Sturbridge, Mass., 1.25.82; Donald and Anne Wing.

term that was set by law at seven years. American apprenticeships tended to be governed more by custom and tradition than by law, and their duration varied. In Virginia, apprenticeships normally ranged from five to seven years.

Apprenticeship contracts required the young man to obey his master, serve him faithfully, avoid temptations of the flesh, and safeguard the "arts and mysteries" of his trade from outsiders. In return, the master promised to teach his apprentice the skills of his trade, oversee his moral development, provide him with food and clothing, and, in some cases, see that he was taught reading and basic arithmetic. Both master and apprentice benefitted from this arrangement. The master was guaranteed a cheap

source of labor which, while at first unskilled, became progressively more productive. The apprentice acquired the skills and often many of the tools he needed to earn a living.

An important part of learning a trade was learning to use its tools. Initially, the apprentice learned to do the rough, relatively simple jobs of his occupation while he ran errands, cleaned the shop, and watched the more experienced men work. As he grew in strength, stamina, knowledge, skill, and judgment, the apprentice took on more complicated jobs that required him to use more demanding tools.

Many of the skills an apprentice acquired were mechanical ones. He learned to use rules, squares, compasses, and gauges to lay out the

46. Many tools were simple but quite effective. This scribe is from the Nixon tool chest. It is for marking lines and consists of a saddler's awl blade mounted in a roughly shaped oak handle. OL: 4 7/8". Courtesy of the Framingham Historical and Natural History Society, Framingham, Mass.

designs of his work accurately. The master showed him that a line cut with a knife was more precise than one drawn with a pencil. He was taught how to use particular tools to shape parts and cut joints, as well as when and where certain joints were most appropriate. He learned how to maintain tools and keep them sharp, essential tasks that he would repeat everyday throughout his career. And he became familiar with working techniques that reduced the chances of personal injury.

The apprentice also gained an understanding of wood. He learned to recognize various types and to select pieces with the proper characteristics for the job at hand. He soon began to develop an almost instinctive feel for his materials and how to apply tools to them in the most effective way.

Experience taught the young craftsman how to judge distances, angles, and spaces by eye and touch as well as by measure. His master shared with him his knowledge of special jigs, shortcuts, and tricks that eased the work, as well as formulas for glues, stains, and finishes. The young man also learned productive work routines and became aware of how an efficient shop

47. Sharpening stones were natural stones, often irregularly shaped. Surfaces were contoured for special tasks such as honing carving tools. These are from the Cartwright kit and probably date before 1810. Clockwise from upper left: G1986-268, 121, 118, 116, 115, 117, and 109, gift of Frank M. Smith. The drawknife may be by John Ellis of Sheffield (1787–1817), who, while listed as a knifemaker, had a very similar mark. OL: 15 1/2". Courtesy of the Paul B. Kebabian Collection. The carving tools are by John Butterworth of Sheffield (1774–1787). 1991-155; 1990-116.

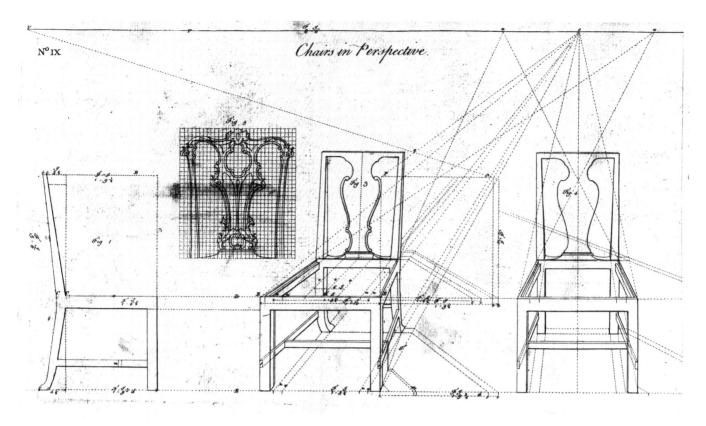

48. Thomas Chippendale stressed that cabinetmakers needed to understand perspective drawing and rules of classical proportion to design their products successfully. Plate IX from *The Gentleman and Cabinetmaker's Director,* 1st ed. (London, 1754).

was laid out and run, how to purchase raw materials and hardware, and how to deal with customers.

Design skills also were important. Some artisans produced wares that followed time-honored patterns, but others made products with only the most general guidance from their customers or produced goods for which they hoped to find buyers later. Successful craftsmen had to know where to obtain designs and how to translate them into three-dimensional results. Drawing was an important skill for visualizing products, giving instructions to employees, and communicating with customers about design possibilities. Most American woodworkers probably were not masters of the theoretical aspects of proportion and design emphasized in published books of architectural and furniture patterns, but almost all were familiar with basic formulas for producing visually successful re-

sults by stepping off proportions using compasses or measuring devices such as the carpenter's ten-foot pole. Although more abstract, the "tools" of running a business and product design were just as important to the self-employed artisan as saws and chisels.

English guild regulations required that a formal apprenticeship be completed before an artisan was permitted to practice his trade independently as a master craftsman. Although Norfolk, Virginia, and possibly other colonial cities enforced similar restrictions on tradesmen, in general, anyone with the financial means to do so could go into business for himself in America. Many woodworkers never acquired the capital to set up their own businesses and worked for others throughout their lives. For those who did set up shops, however, success was determined by the artisan's trade skills, business acumen, and ability to attract customers with good quality, useful, attractive, and reasonably priced products. If he wished to compete with his fellow woodworkers and earn a decent living, a tradesman also had to make wares as efficiently as possible. Much of what he had learned as an apprentice was designed to increase his speed and ensure his ability to produce goods to acceptable standards. In addition to a willingness to apply his skills industriously, however, an artisan needed the proper tools. Implements designed to perform the tasks at hand assisted him in achieving both product quality and production efficiency.

Many woodworking processes could be accomplished using general-purpose tools like axes, saws, chisels, and marking and measuring devices. Other tasks—such as cutting complex moldings, boring specially shaped holes, or intricate carving—required or were drastically simplified by the use of more specialized implements. Some tools combined multiple functions. A rabbet plane with a small knife mounted ahead of its main blade automatically scored the wood fibers before it planed them away, resulting in a clean cut across grain. To achieve the same quality cut with an ordinary rabbet plane required that the woodworker first make a saw cut to sever the grain. Other specialized tools eased work by reducing the risk involved in performing certain tasks. Many incorporated fences that guided them or stops that controlled their cutting depth. Simple jigs like miter boxes automatically guided saws at forty-five-degree angles. These "smart tools" reduced the tedium and skill needed to make products. They were welcome, not only because they meant that less-skilled workers could produce better results, but also because they allowed even the most highly skilled artisan to make his wares more efficiently.

Many specialized tools designed to work wood in particular ways were suited only for specific tasks. Tools for making barrels were superbly designed to split out, shape, and join staves of oak but were of little use for dovetailing together a mahogany chest of drawers. Making case furniture required tools seldom

used in coopering: squares, dovetail saws, and molding planes. Similarly, sawing logs into boards required pitsaws or sawmills, turning necessitated a lathe, and tiny planes, gauges, and drills were needed to make musical instruments. An artisan could acquire new tools to perform new tasks, but in general his kit was chosen because the tools in it permitted him to undertake a specific group of related processes.

Almost all competent woodworkers were highly skilled by modern standards; however, the nature of their skills varied considerably. To use a broad ax to square a log rapidly, an artisan needed not only strength and endurance, but knowledge about the characteristics of his wood

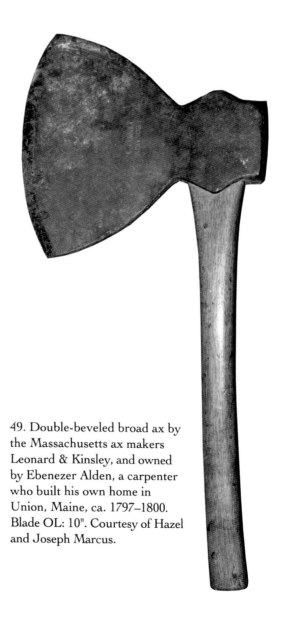

49. Double-beveled broad ax by the Massachusetts ax makers Leonard & Kinsley, and owned by Ebenezer Alden, a carpenter who built his own home in Union, Maine, ca. 1797–1800. Blade OL: 10". Courtesy of Hazel and Joseph Marcus.

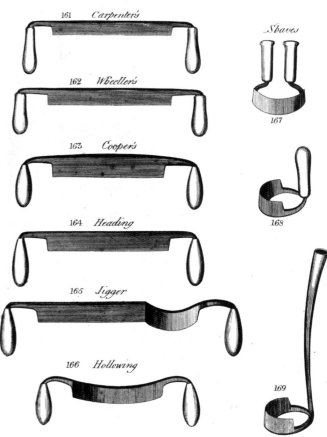

DRAWING KNIVES

161 *Carpenter's*

162 *Wheeler's*

163 *Cooper's*

164 *Heading*

165 *Jigger*

166 *Hollowing*

Shaves

167

168

169

50. Specialized tools of the cooper were illustrated in Joseph Smith's *Explanation or Key, to the Various Manufactories of Sheffield*, a catalog of Sheffield products printed in 1816. Courtesy of Gene W. Kijowski.

and a well-tuned ability to make each cut precisely along a predetermined line. The creation of flat boards using a jack plane or the shaping of a cabriole leg with saw, drawknife, and spokeshave required other types of judgment and skill. Experience using one group of tools did not automatically equip an artisan to use others.

Since no artisan could own every tool and master every skill, woodworking had long been divided into trades, each of which had a distinctive group of tools, skills, and products. During the eighteenth century, the growing demand for

products and their increasing complexity resulted in further divisions. Specialists acquired the tools and skills needed to accomplish a narrow range of work as efficiently as possible. As in the tool industry, these woodworkers often cooperated to make goods more rapidly, cheaply, and better than individual craftsmen using general-purpose tools and skills. This trend was most apparent in locations where the market for goods was large enough to support a high level of production. In England, for example, London furniture makers began to special-

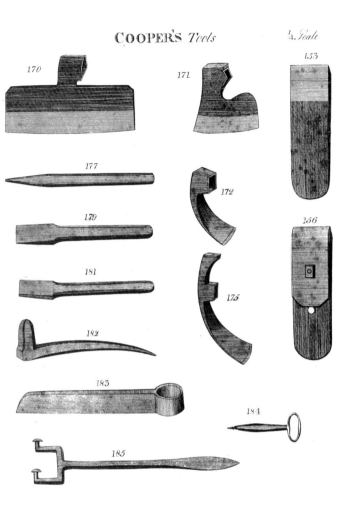

COOPER'S *Tools*   ¼ *Scale*

170 171 153
177 172 156
179 175
181
182
183 184
185

ize in case pieces, chairs, or bedsteads. Within a shop, distinct processes like case making, turning, carving, veneering, upholstery, and finishing could be divided among specially trained and equipped artisans.

Such narrow specialization occurred much less frequently in America. American artisans usually had access to considerably smaller markets than their English urban counterparts, and while American cities might support carvers, turners, or upholsterers, there was a limited demand for most forms of highly specialized

work. Artisans had to make a variety of wares to earn a living. Productivity was important, but diverse kits of tools were more useful than narrowly focused ones. Most woodworkers in Virginia—carpenters and joiners, coopers, cabinetmakers, turners, shipbuilders, and wheelwrights—also tended to support themselves by providing goods and services that did not compete directly with imported wares. Their tool kits were intended to build boats and ships, construct buildings, make products that were difficult or expensive to ship such as furniture, wagons, and agricultural implements, or to produce wares like containers for tobacco for which there was a special local demand.

In rural areas where markets were smaller still, earning a living required yet more diversity. Woodworkers in these areas bridged even the most basic occupational divisions and did everything from building barns and houses to making furniture and wagons and repairing agricultural equipment. Some combined woodworking with farming to make ends meet. While these jacks-of-all-trades owned a variety of tools, their kits probably had little depth and contained few highly specialized tools, a fact that often was reflected in the efficiency and sometimes even the quality of their work.

Despite the relatively unspecialized nature of most American woodworking trades, few products of any complexity were made from start to finish by one person. Within larger shops, although production was not formally undertaken by recognized subtrades, it probably was organized so that certain jobs repeatedly fell to the same people. One man might tend to make wheels, while another fashioned wagon beds. In a cabinet shop, one worker made most of the chairs, a second undertook turned work, and a third concentrated on case pieces.

Unless a woodworker was very isolated, he also participated in a network of specialists that spanned the Atlantic. He bought tools made by toolmakers in Sheffield, nails and hardware made by smiths and founders in Birmingham, resins and pigments for finishes prepared by colormen in London, and fabric and

51. A desk and bookcase made in Williamsburg about 1770. While Williamsburg cabinetmakers shaped, joined, and finished the piece's wooden components, it incorporated the products of glassmakers, weavers, manufacturers of furniture hardware, and glue and finish makers in England, mahogany harvesters in the Caribbean, and sawyers of local wood. 1978-9.

glass manufactured by other English specialists. Many craftsmen bought lumber from the local lumber merchant or sawmill rather than cutting it themselves. Materials like mahogany, other exotic woods, and paint pigments came from as far away as the West Indies, South America, and Africa.

Working wood by hand was not a romantic, leisurely pursuit. Many woodworkers no doubt took pride in their occupation and their skills. They must have experienced the satisfaction that comes from working in harmony with a unique piece of wood—and every piece is unique—to transform it with smoothly functioning tools into a crisply shaped product. But earning a living constantly required artisans to balance the quality of their work with the quantity of their production. A combination of skills, productive routines, and effective tools enabled woodworkers to produce their wares with remarkable efficiency. A small team of carpenters and joiners could prepare materials and build an elaborate frame house in less than a year. Between 1768 and 1775 Charleston, South Carolina, cabinetmaker Thomas Elfe, who employed six craftsmen, sold 1,552 pieces of furniture ranging from elaborate desks and bookcases to rudimentary stools.[40] The account books of Philadelphia chairmaker Solomon Fussell indicate that he purchased over 5,000 chair parts from one turner during a five and one-half month period in 1739–1740.[41] Nineteenth-century London window sash makers working by hand considered making a pair of sashes to be a reasonable day's work.[42] More recently, twentieth-century coopers working with eighteenth-century-style tools were expected to make one large (108 or 128 gallon), two medium (18 gallon), or four small (4 1/2 gallon) barrels in an eight-hour day, and Colonial Williamsburg turners can transform a rough blank into an elaborate stair baluster in six to eight minutes.

Almost every form of hand production required hard work. Products were made ax blow by ax blow, plane stroke by plane stroke, chisel cut by chisel cut. Woodworkers had no other way to make their wares, and their efforts were not considered to be exceptional or unusual. The types of tools a craftsman used, however, often determined the particular labors and rhythms of his workday life.

The men who cut down trees, hewed them into beams, and sawed or split them into rails, shingles, or boards performed some of the heaviest work. If lumbering or sawing was their sole occupation, they spent day after day swinging axes or pulling and pushing heavy saws. They handled large pieces of timber and extremely sharp tools, and one error in judgment could result in serious injury. Most worked outdoors, exposed to extremes of hot and cold as well as rain, sleet, and snow. Their bodies adjusted to this repetitive work and their endurance was astounding, but their labor was rigorous.

Coopers, wheelwrights, shipwrights, carpenters, and millwrights also worked with large, heavy products that demanded strength and endurance. While more varied than the labor of sawyers and woodcutters, their work involved laborious and repetitive tasks. Newspaper advertisements for runaway slaves and servants who practiced these trades indicate that they too were exposed to injury from axes, adzes, and other edge tools. Even those who worked under cover often did so in unheated, drafty shops.

Joiners, cabinetmakers, turners, musical instrument makers, and other tradesmen who made smaller objects worked under the best conditions. Their tools were lighter and less liable to inflict serious injuries. They most often worked in enclosed shops since the manufacture of their products required a modicum of cleanliness. Their work was lighter and more varied, but even so, it often was repetitive. Tedious, close work subjected them to eyestrain, and many were exposed to carcinogenic wood dust and toxic fumes from finishing materials.

Tool capabilities and the skill and effort required to use particular implements also influenced artisans' *attitudes* toward their work, including acceptable levels of physical exertion. Hazards attendant to tool use determined common health and safety risks. The conditions

52. Pitsawing logs into boards was laborious, monotonous work that nevertheless also demanded skill and constant attention. From *The Book of Trades,* an English publication reprinted in Philadelphia and Richmond, Virginia, in 1807 and reprinted as *The Little Book of Early American Crafts and Trades* in 1976.

53. A cooper at work. Transfer print on a Staffordshire creamware jug, ca. 1795. OH: 8". 1992-224.

54. *The Carpenter's Shop at Forty Hill, Enfield*, ca. 1813, by John Hill (1779–1841), oil on canvas, England. Both Hill and his father were carpenters, and this painting probably depicts their shop. Although architectural details and the pastoral setting of this shop are decidedly English, the tools, shop arrangement, and work at hand probably differed little from many American shops. English carpenters traditionally used woven baskets like the one in the left foreground to carry tools to jobs away from the shop. Courtesy of the Trustees of the Tate Gallery, Millbank, London.

under which particular tools were best used influenced shop layouts, work routines, and daily schedules. A carving bench might be located by a window to take advantage of good light, while one for rough planing could be placed elsewhere. Work was organized so that tasks could be done repetitively, reducing time wasted in constantly changing tools, setups, and the artisan's focus. Ultimately, a good day's work was defined by how fast a woodsman could fell trees with an ax or a cooper could shape staves with a drawknife.

The intimate connection between eighteenth-century tools and trades naturally led to their use as symbols. Painters and printmakers used distinctive tools to identify the trades of their subjects. A cooper carried a cooper's adze or ax, while carpenters were universally identified by the two-foot rules protruding from the pockets of their breeches. On trade signs and trade cards, tools announced to prospective customers an artisan's skills and the goods he offered for sale. In parades and processions, craftsmen frequently bore "implements suitable to their several occupations" to identify themselves to spectators.[43] Tools were also used allegorically. For Freemasons, the level symbolized equality, the plumb uprightness, and the

Tools: Working Wood in Eighteenth-Century America

55. In *The Carpenter's Yard*, ca. 1725, oil on canvas, England, by Jack Laguerre (d. 1748, formerly attributed to William Hogarth) nearly every workman carries a folding two-foot rule in his pocket. There is no doubt about who is the customer, the master builder, and the workman. Courtesy of Sidney F. Sabin.

56. This Master's Chair of an unidentified Virginia Masonic Lodge was made by Benjamin Bucktrout of Williamsburg during the late 1760s. It is decorated with symbolic tools of Freemasonry, among them a folding rule, a pair of compasses, a square, a mallet, plumbs, and a level. 1983-317.

square true virtue. In a print, a pair of compasses might remind proper young ladies and gentlemen to keep within the circumscribed spheres of acceptable public and private behavior. Ultimately, tools, which represented physical labor, symbolized the status of the working men and women who used them. In the social hierarchy of eighteenth-century America, those who worked with their hands, while respected for their abilities, only rarely attained the coveted status of the leisured "lady" or "gentleman." Tools and their use literally and figuratively defined many of the boundaries of the artisan's daily existence.

57. *Keep Within Compass.* detail, hand-colored line and mezzotint engraving, England, 1785. 1958-629, 1.

Tools: Working Wood in Eighteenth-Century America

Tools and Products

Given unlimited time, patience, and motivation, a skilled woodworker can create almost any product using the most rudimentary hand tools. The better suited the tools are to performing the individual operations involved, however, the easier and more efficient the entire process becomes.

In practice, there is almost always a give-and-take relationship between products and the tools used to make them. On the one hand, the capabilities of existing tools and their accustomed uses influence the design and construction of products. On the other, consumer demands for more, improved, or new products motivate toolmakers to create tools and artisans to develop new tool-using techniques to facili-

tate the manufacture of these products. Both of these forces were at work in the seventeenth and eighteenth centuries.

Changing fashions influenced the ways in which tools developed. As consumers came to desire more elaborate and highly finished furniture during the late seventeenth century, some artisans began to specialize in making the new styles. These craftsmen, called cabinetmakers, made case furniture by dovetailing together wide boards rather than using older panel-and-frame methods of construction favored by joiners. This innovation and the decorative techniques that accompanied it prompted the refinement of many tools. Finer work required finer saws; new tools were developed to cut and apply

58. Tools for applying veneer: a gluepot for keeping glue warm, a toothing plane by George Mutter (1766–1799) of London for preparing surfaces for gluing, and a veneer hammer, a tool used like a squeegee for seating and smoothing the veneer. Plane OL: 7 1/2". 1986-114; 1982-140; G1986-268, 148, gift of Frank M. Smith.

veneers. Carving tools and molding planes were produced to ease the creation of fashionable decoration.

Technological advances in other areas of manufacturing also stimulated the development of new woodworking tools. When better glass became available late in the seventeenth century, it led to the introduction of double-hung sash windows whose framework was constructed entirely of wood. This innovation prompted the invention of new sash-making tools. The window-making trade, which before had been concerned largely with fitting small panes of glass into lead strips, changed completely. On a more purely technical level, the ready availability of woodscrews created a need for screwdrivers, and the growing use of bolts and nuts for the construction of machines required that some woodworkers equip themselves with wrenches.

Despite these developments, most wooden products reflected a balance between customers' desires, the practical capabilities of existing tools, and artisans' skills and approaches to their work. If a consumer wanted a wooden chair, he had numerous choices. He could buy a ladderback chair made primarily of cylindrical parts, select a Windsor chair, or choose an even more formal side chair with straight or cabriole legs. The characteristics of each type of chair required that a different tool kit be used in its construction. The cylindrical parts of the ladderback chair were most easily produced by a turner's chisels and gouges as the wood spun on a lathe. Making the chair's splats required several saws and a plane. Its seat lists were formed with a drawknife. The Windsor chair also had some turned parts, but shaping its seat, spindles, and bow involved the use of saws, a

59. A chair consisting primarily of parts shaped on a lathe. Rappahannock River Basin of Virginia, 1750–1790. OH: 39 7/8". 1992-24.

60. Windsor chairs consisted of parts turned on a lathe and those made by sawing, adzing, planing, and shaving. Connecticut, ca. 1790. OH: 38 3/8". 1952-173.

61. Formal sidechairs were constructed using much more time-consuming techniques for shaping, joining, and decorating their parts. Williamsburg, ca. 1775. OH: 38 7/8". G1965-184, gift of William Byron Bailey in memory of Dorothy King Bailey.

62. Few American lathes dating to the early nineteenth century or before are known. This homemade—but elaborate—English lathe has a mechanism that allows it to be used to cut threads on wood. The treadle and flywheel mechanism can be shifted from side to side to align the drive with the headstock. Attributed to William Walters of Bassingbourn, Hertfordshire (dated 1804). G1988-14, acquired through the generosity of Martyl and Emil Pollak.

curved drawknife or adze, a straight drawknife and spokeshave, and several types of planes. The flat and curved parts of the more formal side chair—many of them joined at complex angles—could be made only by first sawing them to rough shape and then bringing them to final form with planes, shaves, chisels, gouges, and backsaws. While a few shops made all of these types of chairs, most specialized in one kind only. Once a customer decided which style he wanted, he chose a shop that had the tools and skills to produce it. Style was probably a major factor in the customer's choice, but price was also important. Turning was a very fast way to produce parts, so turned chairs were the

cheapest. Making Windsor chairs required a more diverse kit of tools, involved a broader range of skills, and required more time. They sold for slightly more. Joined side chairs were the most expensive, since it took larger tool kits, more versatile skills, more exacting workmanship, and considerably more time to produce them.

The cost of a product was based upon the materials and time needed for its production. Decorated products usually required more labor than similar undecorated ones, so decoration often became a sign of quality. The relationship between tools, labor, and decoration was not always obvious, however. Pierced chair

Tools and Products

63. A blanket chest made by a cabinetmaker in the Shenandoah Valley of Virginia about 1775. OW: 48". 1938-155.

64. A blanket chest made by a house joiner on the Eastern Shore of Virginia about 1770. OW: 56". 1930-108.

Tools: Working Wood in Eighteenth-Century America

splats, moldings, inlay, and carving required significant time and labor to produce, but making some ornate forms was faster and easier than creating other, seemingly less complex, ones. Complex decorative shapes could be turned quickly on a lathe, for instance, and it took much less time to turn the balusters and reels or bamboo shapes of Windsor chair legs than to saw and plane the surfaces of the much "simpler" rectangular ones found on more formal chairs.

The customer's choice of a particular type of product determined the basic nature of the tool kit used to make it, but the specific tools available to the artisan and his personal ways of using them often influenced the details of his wares. Individual artisans had to adapt to the demands of their customers for new and different products, which occasionally meant obtaining and learning to use new tools. The rote training received by most woodworkers, however, inclined them to be conservative. The comfort of using familiar tools and practiced skills encouraged them to follow traditional methods and approaches to design and construction. Many of the tool improvements made during the century reflected this conservatism. They made old tasks easier rather than permitting the performance of new ones. Despite the introduction of new fashions in woodwork and its decoration in the eighteenth century, the basic technology for working wood changed little.

At the most fundamental level, an artisan's tool kit influenced his choice of materials. Some woods were selected for their decorative appeal or structural qualities, while others were chosen because they were best suited to shaping with particular tools. Maple turned easily and often was used for turned chair legs. Besides being strong and durable, oak could be split readily into boards and rails, making it ideal for barrels and wagon parts. Pine could be sawn, planed, and carved more quickly than many other woods and was used for house interiors. The popularity of walnut and mahogany for furniture was prompted not only by their visual appeal but also by the precision with which these woods could be decorated with planed moldings and intricate carving.

An artisan's tools and skills also affected his approach to design and construction. A blanket chest made on Virginia's Eastern Shore provides an interesting example of what could happen when an artisan trained in one trade and equipped with its tools was called upon to make products usually produced by another. Most eighteenth-century blanket chests were made using cabinetmaking techniques: flat boards were dovetailed together to form a box to which a top and feet were added (fig. 63). Although it has the same basic form, the Eastern Shore piece in figure 64 apparently was made by a craftsman whose tools and training led him to prefer the house joinery techniques of panel-and-frame construction.

The tools woodworkers used also influenced what they produced in more subtle ways. Since individual artisans repeatedly used patterns, molding planes, and other tools that produced predetermined shapes, their products, while not exactly alike, often had similar features. Instead of designing each set of wheels or wagon parts anew, wheelwrights generally made several standard types whose components could be quickly laid out using existing templates and gauges. House joiners and cabinetmakers tended to decorate their products with the molding planes they owned, which represented only a small selection of those available. The shapes of chisels and gouges in a carver's tool kit influenced the layout and execution of the scrolls, volutes, and other elements he carved. As long as the overall product was satisfactory, it appears that consumers accepted these idiosyncratic results of an artisan's techniques and tool kit without question.

Techniques and designs were standardized for other reasons as well. Standardization allowed craftsmen to produce components in batches, stockpiling parts for future use. It was also important if one person prepared the raw materials or components and another worked them up into finished products. The advantages of standardized products encouraged many shops to offer their wares in incremental price ranges. A "standard" piece of furniture or room interior was offered at a given price, and customers were charged additional set amounts for extra elaboration or decoration.

While some standardization was intentionally introduced to ease labor or speed production, in other cases it just happened. Apprentices taught by the same master tended to use the same tools and methods to make things in similar, tried-and-true ways. Workers who shared tools or learned skills from one another also shared techniques. Consumers tended to prefer the same styles and designs as their neighbors. These common approaches and preferences encouraged the production of stylistically and technically similar wares. Eastern Virginia's carpenters and joiners built houses with framing details different from those used in the backcountry and its cabinetmakers commonly employed construction techniques rarely found elsewhere in America. Thus the structure and decoration of an object often indicate where and by whom it was made.

Ultimately, even standards of quality were influenced by the tools artisans used. Consumers wanted the things they bought to be made in a good and workmanlike—a professional—manner. From a practical standpoint, both artisans and consumers judged the quality of eighteenth-century wheels, barrels, boats, and tables by the standard of the best wheel, barrel, boat, or table that could be made with the tools and skills available.

The practical capabilities of tools also influenced consumers' expectations regarding other product characteristics such as the uniformity of details. Skilled artisans using eighteenth-century woodworking tools could produce extremely precise work even by modern standards, but the effort required varied with the type of tool used. Some tools like molding planes tended to produce consistent results automatically. Use of these "tools of certainty" promoted accuracy, so producing a long run of identical molding was relatively quick and easy.[44] Using chisels and gouges to carve identical mantels or chair legs was much more difficult and time consuming. Both consumers' and artisans' expectations varied from product to product.

Craftsmen and customers usually agreed about how best to apply labor. When precision was important to the mechanical quality of a

65. Pear Valley, a mid-eighteenth-century house in Northampton County, Virginia (Eastern Shore), has a tilted false plate that carries the rafters. This construction technique is a distinctive characteristic of house framing found in the Chesapeake and areas influenced by it. Photography by William J. Graham. Pear Valley is owned by the Association for the Preservation of Virginia Antiquities.

66. While apparently all the same at a casual glance, closer inspection of these stair balusters from the George Wythe House in Williamsburg reveals that both the turner and his customer were satisfied with "close enough"—a standard that varied depending upon the product.

Tools: Working Wood in Eighteenth-Century America

67. Hidden surfaces were often left unfinished to save the artisan's time and his customer's money. The visible tool marks and rough surfaces on the normally unseen portions of this mid-eighteenth-century Pennsylvania side chair contrast sharply with its finely finished exterior. 1967-602.

product, the conscientious craftsman took the time to work to exacting standards. The effort he expended upon the precision or finish of other features, however, was much more selective. The tools used in smoothing and finishing wood, for example, dictated that these processes be performed in stages to produce increasingly flatter and smoother surfaces. The artisan could stop the process at a number of points. Utilitarian objects generally were less highly finished than finer ones. The visible surfaces of high-quality furniture were carefully carried through the entire smoothing process, while unseen surfaces were left much less finished. Products meant to be seen up close or handled were normally executed more carefully than those meant to be seen from a distance. Archi-

tectural carving was rarely as precise as furniture carving. Small drawers for a desk interior were more precisely made than the larger drawers below.

Similar considerations governed the selection of materials. The visible surfaces of high-style furniture often were made of fine hardwoods, while softwoods such as pine or poplar were used for drawer interiors, case backs, and other hidden parts. These woods were less expensive and easier to shape. The selective use of labor and materials saved time and effort. These choices, which were often influenced by an artisan's tools, allowed him to give his customer the most impressive product for the money.

It is unlikely that many artisans pondered the abstract connections between their tools,

68. Woods for normally unseen surfaces were selected to save both time and the expense of raw materials. Desk and bookcase attributed to Peter Scott of Williamsburg, ca. 1760. Walnut and yellow pine. 1976-95.

69. Although the final form and quality of a product was first and foremost the result of the customer's desires and purse and the woodworker's talent and skill, the capabilities of tools influenced both consumer expectations and the specific methods of the artisan's execution. *A Cabinet Maker's Office,* oil on canvas, England, ca. 1770. Courtesy of the Board of Trustees of the Victoria and Albert Museum, London.

Tools: Working Wood in Eighteenth-Century America

their products, and their customers' expectations. Tools were merely the everyday stuff of life for most eighteenth-century American woodworkers. Artisans took them in hand when needed, and left them behind when they went to dinner. Only rarely did they think about who made their tools, where they came from, or how their tools placed them in the larger context of history. Still, when handling an old tool, it is hard to ignore the well-worn spots where fingers fell over two centuries ago. Few survivals from the past bear such compelling witness to the life of the common man and to the world in which he labored.

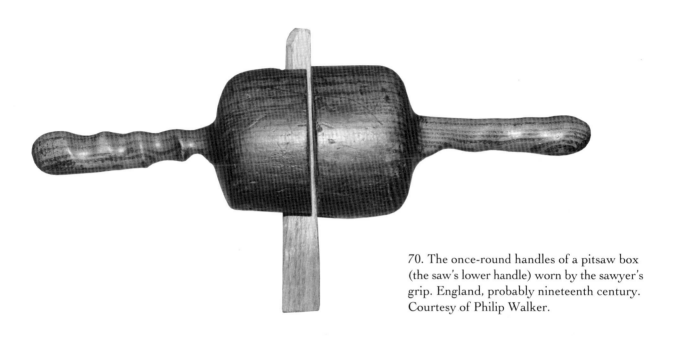

70. The once-round handles of a pitsaw box (the saw's lower handle) worn by the sawyer's grip. England, probably nineteenth century. Courtesy of Philip Walker.

A Pictorial Essay of Selected Eighteenth- and Early Nineteenth-Century Woodworking Tools

Eighteenth-century Continental writers described and illustrated the tools and craft techniques used by artisans in their countries. Such monumental works as Diderot's *Encyclopédie* (Paris, 1751–1765), Andre Jacob Roubo's *L'Art du Menuisier* [The Art of the Joiner] (Paris, 1769–1775) (part of the Arts and Trades series published by the French Royal Academy of Sciences), and Peter Nathanael Sprengel's *Handwerke und Künste* [Trades and Arts] (Berlin, 1767–1777) contained detailed information about woodworking implements.

Unfortunately, the English and their American colonists did not follow suit. During the late seventeenth century, Joseph Moxon described tools and techniques used in carpentry, joinery, and turning in his *Mechanick Exercises, or the Doctrine of Handy-Works* (published in London as a series beginning in 1677), and Randle Holme illustrated and described tools in his *Academy of Armory* (Chester, 1688). From that point until about 1800, however, there were few published descriptions or illustrations of English or American woodworking tools that updated Moxon and Holme or contained additional tool-related information, other than the engravings that occasionally appeared on English toolmakers' and dealers' trade cards. As a result, modern-day American collectors and craftsmen have often turned to Continental writers to learn about early tools.

Unless Continental material is used carefully, it can be misleading. Eighteenth-century English and Continental woodworkers often employed similar methods; however, while similar in function, English and Continental tools often differed. In some cases the differences were in minor details of shaping; in others, the stylistic design and even the mechanical features of English tools were distinctive.

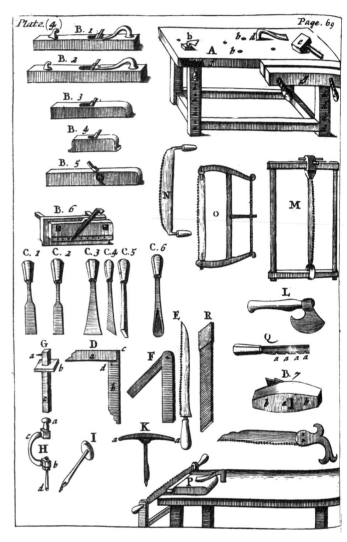

71. Tools of the joiner. Plate 4 from Joseph Moxon's *Mechanick Exercises* (London, 1703 edition). Although Moxon's text describes English trade practices, he copied most of these tool illustrations from a contemporary French source.

Too few tools survive from the seventeenth century and before to warrant definite conclusions, but it is likely that the distinctive styles of many English tools developed largely during the seventeenth and eighteenth centu-

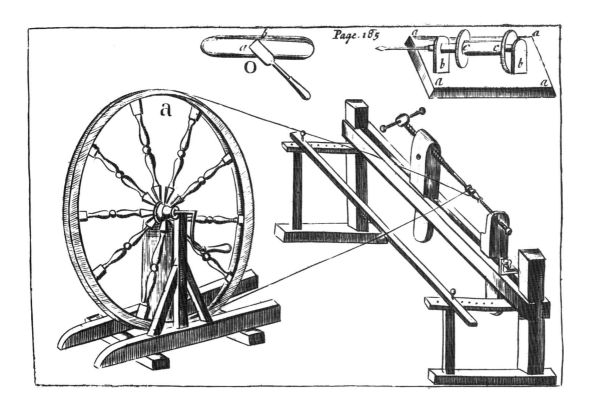

72. A lathe powered by a hand-cranked "great wheel." Plate 14
from Joseph Moxon's *Mechanick Exercises* (London, 1703 edition).

ries. Before then, many English artisans probably used a combination of locally made tools and tools (especially edge tools) imported from the Continent, where trades were generally more advanced. There was also a relatively unrestricted flow of artisans and manufactured goods between England and the mainland. At the beginning of the seventeenth century, while some English-made tools reflected local designs, there may have been little difference between saws, chisels, plane blades, and other tools used by many English woodworkers and their western Continental contemporaries. Tools recovered from the silt along the Thames River in London and probably dating from the sixteenth and seventeenth centuries, as well as implements from early seventeenth-century archaeological sites in Virginia, if not actually Continental, were strongly influenced by Continental designs.

Throughout the seventeenth century, England distanced itself from Continental Europe in the wake of the English Reformation and as a result of increasingly protectionist trade policies. Continental tools undoubtedly continued to influence the development of woodworking implements in England through trade, the immigration of artisans from Europe, and English preferences for fashionable woodwork inspired by Continental styles. Yet by the mid-eighteenth century, demand for domestic manufactures of all types, the growth of the English iron and steel industries, and the rise of the toolmaking industry resulted in tools whose designs, while blending both local and Continental traditions (a "western European" tradition), were influenced more heavily by local technical and stylistic preferences and manufacturing capabilities than by Continental models. Despite the immense variety of tool types produced by En-

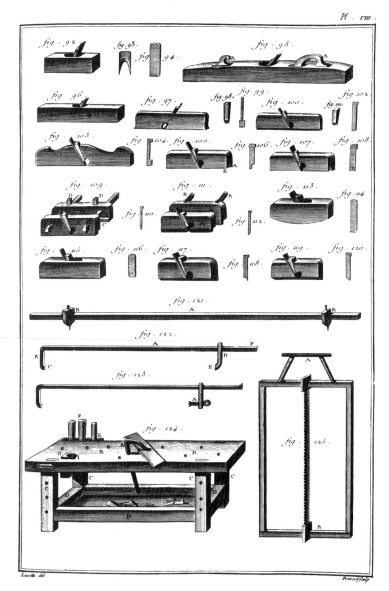

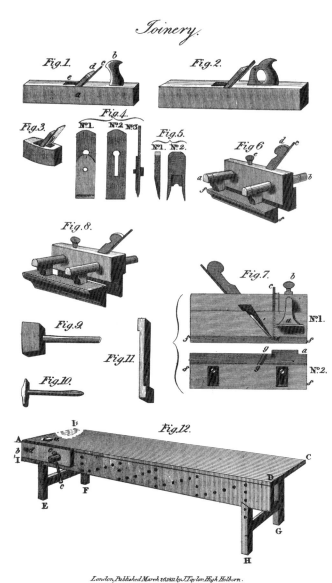

73. French joiner's tools illustrated in Diderot's *Ency-clopédie* (Paris, 1769).

74. English joiner's tools illustrated in Peter Nicholson's *Mechanical Exercises* (London, 1812). Although many of these tools were used for the same functions as those illustrated in Diderot, note the differences in their designs.

glish makers in the eighteenth century, shared design details, as well as a less definable, but nonetheless real common character, frequently distinguish English tools from those made elsewhere.

Surviving eighteenth-century tools and illustrations found in late eighteenth-century tool catalogs indicate that most English tool designs were straightforward and derived from tools'

functions. The tools have little of the decorative elaboration such as scrolled handles, carving, and decorative file work found on many Continental examples. The extra finishing touches on English tools—carefully shaped handles, brass ferrules, octagonal bolsters, and chamfered edges on planes—usually were incorporated because they made the tools more comfortable to use, more durable, or, in some cases, easier to man-

Tools: Working Wood in Eighteenth-Century America

75. Seventeenth-century handsaw and riveting hammer head excavated in Virginia. The handsaw originally was fitted with a wooden pistol-grip handle. These tools are either Continental, probably Dutch, or are English tools that bear a greater resemblance to forms popular on the Continent than to later, standard English types. If Continental, these tools could have been imported into Virginia directly by Dutch merchants. Similar tools have been found at London archaeological sites. Saw OL: 25", from Jordan's Point, near Hopewell, Virginia, ca. 1620–1635. Courtesy of the Virginia Department of Historic Resources, 44PG302/F-110 EU#766. Hammer from Flowerdew Hundred, also near Hopewell, from a ca. 1690–1730 context. Courtesy of the Flowerdew Hundred Foundation, 44PG66/508A1-53.

76. Dutch jack and panel raising planes (left) and a Germanic combination tongue-and-groove plane. Like many Continental tools, these planes have purely decorative elements such as carving or elaborately shaped handles. The panel raiser and tongue-and-groove plane are dated 1770 and 1787 respectively. Panel raiser OL: 7 7/8", marked FM, with a fleur-de-lis; jack plane stamped AMD; the irons of both are replacements. Courtesy of Martyl and Emil Pollak.

ufacture. Tools made in America based on English models follow this functional approach; however, both they and their English prototypes reveal a well-tuned sense of design on the part of their makers. Many are almost sculptural in form, boldly proportioned and beautiful objects both to look at and to handle. The makers of hand tools were hand tool users themselves, and their sensitivities to their products' uses and desirable working characteristics were reflected in implements that "came to hand" easily and were well suited for long hours of use.

Many English tool types evolved noticeably over the course of the eighteenth century. Some changes were primarily in details of form and eventually resulted in highly standardized types, a phenomenon which may have been largely caused by the increasing regional specialization of the English tool industry. The transfer of the center of edge tool manufacturing from Birmingham to Sheffield during the second half of the century, for example, may have led to changes in edge tool designs. The concentration of edge tool manufacturing in Sheffield from that date onward, and the growth of long-distance marketing using samples and illustrated catalogs, encouraged standardization.

Other changes were prompted by efforts to improve tools' functional qualities. Edge tools were improved by the use of better steels. A new design of plane blade was introduced that eased the planing of woods with twisted grain. Braces were fitted with metal chucks that accepted standardized bits. The spiral or screw auger, a design that was a significant improvement over earlier types, was invented. Planes with adjustable mechanisms that had previously been made of wood were fitted with more accurate and durable metal parts. The variety of tools designed for specialized tasks grew.

A number of these changes appear to have occurred during the third quarter of the eighteenth century. The growth of specialized makers may have been a major factor, but there were technical reasons as well. Improved steels were developed, as was the technology for rolling steel into consistent sheets for saw blades. Better quality brass became more available. Although almost nothing is known about the evolution of toolmaking tools, it is also possible that some of these changes resulted from other improvements in toolmaking technology.

While these trends were taking place in England, American toolmakers were developing tools of their own designs. Although often

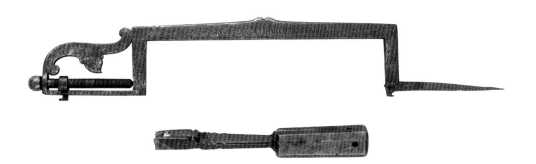

77. A corner chisel, probably German, and a metal cutting saw frame engraved "Henrich[?] Bernhard gemacht 1770." The saw frame was found in Virginia and either was imported to America from a German-speaking region of Europe or made in an area of German settlement in Pennsylvania, Maryland, or Virginia. Chisel OL: 10 1/2". Chisel courtesy of Martyl and Emil Pollak; saw courtesy of the collection of Byron B. Wenger.

Tools: Working Wood in Eighteenth-Century America

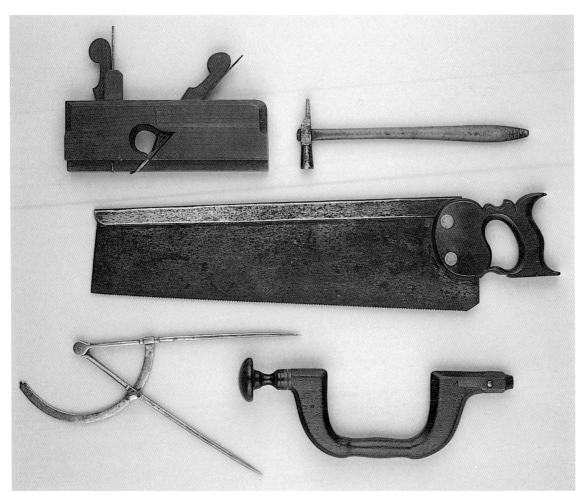

78. Although their shapes often were more purely functional than Continental tools, English implements frequently were beautifully proportioned and boldly executed. Clockwise from upper left: dado plane by John Sym of London (ca. 1775), unmarked riveting hammer (early nineteenth century), saw with illegible maker's mark (mid- to late eighteenth century), brace with its pad (chuck) marked FREETH (probably early nineteenth century), and an unmarked pair of compasses (mid-eighteenth century?). Saw OL: 23". G1986-268, 12, gift of Frank M. Smith; 1952-277, 167; G1986-268, 66, gift of Frank M. Smith; 1992-177; 1992-183.

based largely on English forms, some plane types were made to distinctive American patterns. Other planes reveal an American preference for types that, although made in limited quantity in Britain, were to become standard American forms. They included planes designed to cut simultaneously the molding and rabbet (to receive the glass panes) on the wooden mullions of sash windows and planes for forming raised panels that were longer and designed

somewhat differently than the standard British pattern.

American blacksmiths may have developed a new type of felling ax with a shorter blade and heavier poll (the mass of metal opposite the blade) to make it better balanced. While firmly ascribed to American ax makers by many writers, there is some question about the origin of this form since Virginia store documents suggest that "New England" axes, if indeed they are of this type, were imported into Virginia from both New England and England during the second half of the century. Although the name indicates that they certainly were intended for an American market, there is no clear evidence about where the design originated.

A number of improvements in English tools are documented first in American records. The first known mention of center bits (a broadbladed style for drilling shallow holes) appears in a 1708 Philadelphia estate inventory. The first reference to a brace with a spring to hold interchangeable bits is included in an invoice of tools and goods ordered by George Washington when he was remodeling Mount Vernon in 1759. The earliest documentation of the improved, "double" plane iron and some plane types also are found in American sources.[45] The discovery of information about new tool developments in American rather than English sources may be a reflection of the nature of surviving documentary evidence, but in any case, it suggests that English tools of the most improved and latest designs were readily available to American artisans.

A brief look at several tool types—layout tools for measuring and marking, chisels and gouges, saws, boring tools, and planes—illustrates many of the forms of these tools and the changes and developments they underwent. These types have been selected because numerous documented examples survive. Many fewer examples of other types are known, especially the special purpose tools of trades such as coopering, ship building, and musical instrument making. Where possible, tools are referred to by the names used in Virginia documents.

79. A typical English felling ax of a type found frequently at seventeenth- and eighteenth-century archaeological sites in Virginia. OL: 9 3/4", found at Jamestown, Virginia, in a mid-seventeenth-century context. Courtesy of the National Park Service, Colonial National Historical Park, Jamestown Museum Collection, COLO J-8367-1.

80. An American-pattern felling ax recovered from the wreck of the gunboat *Philadelphia*, sunk on Lake Champlain in 1776. OL: 7". Courtesy of the Smithsonian Institution, Division of Armed Forces History.

Tools: Working Wood in Eighteenth-Century America

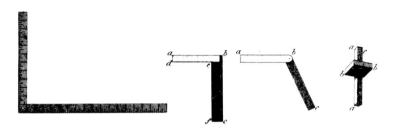

Layout Tools for Measuring and Marking

Eighteenth-century artisans used a variety of tools—compasses and calipers, rules, squares, bevels, gauges, and patterns—to lay out and mark cuts and joints and to transfer designs and measurements from one location to another. Some, like compasses and folding rules, usually were obtained from specialist makers. Wooden squares, gauges, and bevels, however, typically were made by artisans for their own use.

Title illustrations are from Peter Nicholson's *Mechanical Exercises* (London, 1812).

1

CARPENTER'S SQUARES

Squares were used to lay out right angles and to check work to make certain it was square. Iron carpenter's squares were durable tools which, unlike most eighteenth-century squares, were calibrated so that they could be used for measuring as well. Many were imported from England, but iron squares also were made by American blacksmiths. These examples, found in New England and probably American made, are dated 1744, 1781, and 1804. All are 12" by 24". 1744 square courtesy of Edward Ingraham; 1781 and 1804 squares courtesy of the Paul B. Kebabian Collection.

2

FOLDING RULES

The most common measuring tool used by woodworkers was the two-foot folding rule. Folding rules were made commercially in England from at least the seventeenth century. These two styles, a two-leg rule by Christopher Stedman of London and a three-leg rule (the smallest leg of which is brass) by an unknown English maker, were standard eighteenth-century types. Rules often incorporated scales and tables for making mathematical and timber measurement calculations. The consistent dimensions of the boxwood legs of these rules indicate they were planed using carefully constructed jigs, a technique that speeded production and resulted in a more uniform product. Both rules are in nearly new condition. The Stedman rule was included in the Hewlett gentleman's tool chest sold in 1773, and the three-leg rule was found under floorboards of the Sandown, New Hampshire, Meeting House completed in 1774. Stedman rule, 1957-123, A18; Sandown rule courtesy of Malcolm MacGregor.

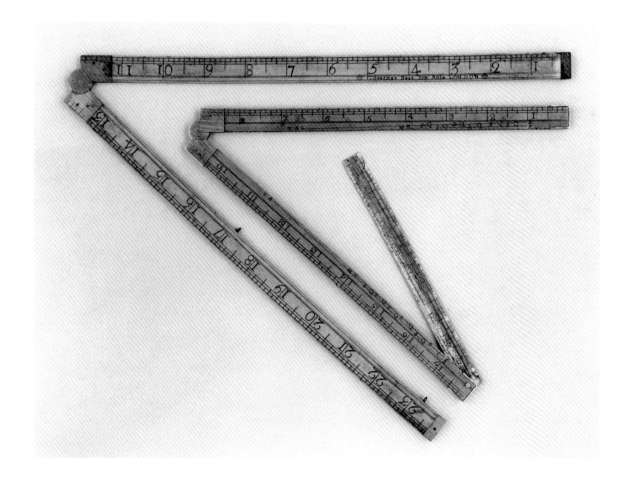

3

HOMEMADE WOODEN SQUARES

Thomas Nixon of Framingham, Massachusetts, made these squares of birch, maple, walnut, and mahogany in the late eighteenth or early nineteenth century. They were used for joinery or cabinetwork. The decorative shaping and nearly equal lengths of the blades and beams are typical of small eighteenth-century squares. The largest is 10 1/4" by 12". Courtesy of the Framingham Historical and Natural History Society, Framingham, Mass.

4

MARKING AND MORTISING GAUGES

Gauges were used to scribe or cut lines parallel to the edge of a board. As the woodworker ran the fence of the gauge along the board edge, one or more small knives mounted at the end of the gauge stem made the desired marks or cuts. Marking gauges (bottom) had single blades and were used to mark the dimensions of cuts for sizing material or positioning joints. Mortise gauges (top) had pairs of blades spaced to match the user's mortise-cutting chisels. They were used to mark the cuts forming mortise-and-tenon joints. Both of these gauges are adjustable, with movable fences locked into place by a wedge or a screw. Woodworkers also made permanently set gauges for often-repeated tasks. The marking gauge is from the Nixon tool group and was made about 1800. OL: 9". The mortise gauge has been repaired with a wrought nail and probably dates to the second half of the eighteenth century. OL: 6 1/4". Marking gauge courtesy of the Framingham Historical and Natural History Society, Framingham, Mass.; mortise gauge courtesy of the Stanley-Whitman House, Farmington, Conn., 200D.2.

Tools: Working Wood in Eighteenth-Century America

5

MARKING GAUGE, TAP, AND SCREW BOX

Thomas Nixon used this tap (upper left) and screw box (right) to cut the threads on the locking screw and fence of his gauge. Courtesy of the Framingham Historical and Natural History Society, Framingham, Mass.

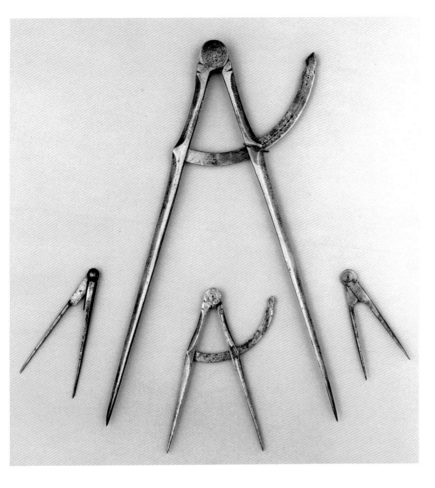

COMPASSES AND CALIPERS

Compasses were used to measure and fit work. The designs of many products were based upon proportional relationships between their parts, which were stepped off with compasses, rather than on measurements calculated in feet and inches. Compasses also were used to draw circles, make geometric calculations, and transfer dimensions from a pattern or workpiece to another location. Calipers resemble compasses, but their legs were curved so that they could be used to gauge the dimensions of round pieces more easily. Birmingham and Lancashire makers produced a variety of compass and caliper designs. These compasses were made during the late eighteenth or early nineteenth century in Birmingham: the large and small "coopers compasses" (center) by Freeth (probably Benjamin), the "square joint" pair (left) by Sam Ault, and the "rule joint" pair (right) by W. & C. Wynn. The largest is 17 7/8" overall. Large cooper's compass, 1987-28; small cooper's compass, 1985-195; square joint compass, 1991-613; rule joint compass, 1987-742.

Some calipers and compasses had a curved "wing" fixed to one leg and sliding through the other. Tightening a set screw on the adjustable leg locked the tool in the desired position. These unmarked calipers probably were made in Birmingham during the late eighteenth or early nineteenth century. OL: 17 1/8". Courtesy of Martyl and Emil Pollak.

7

COMMERCIALLY MADE MARKING GAUGE AND SQUARE

This mahogany marking gauge and brass-bladed square are the earliest known commercially manufactured English examples. They are from the 1773 Hewlett chest and were probably made in London. As the English tool industry expanded during the second half of the eighteenth century, commercial toolmakers began to produce more types of layout tools. Early examples like these closely resemble their homemade counterparts, although small homemade squares rarely had metal blades. The brass blade of this square would have made it an unusual luxury. Gauge OL: 6 7/8". 1957-123, A5 and A17.

8

BEVELS

Bevels were used to lay out angles other than ninety degrees. Some were fixed at commonly used angles, such as forty-five degrees. Others, like these, were adjustable. They were useful for transferring an already established angle to a workpiece that had to be cut to the same shape. These bevels were made about 1800 or slightly later. The homemade bevel on the left is all beech. The middle tool was commercially manufactured and has a mahogany stock and an iron or steel blade. The bevel on the right also has an iron or steel blade but was strengthened and made more attractive by the addition of brass wear plates to its mahogany stock. By the late eighteenth century, other commercially made layout tools also began to incorporate such refinements. This trend toward producing more elaborate and decorative tools was to be a hallmark of both the English and American toolmaking industries in the nineteenth century. The blade of the middle bevel is 9 1/16" long. Left to right: G1986-268, 60 and 59, gift of Frank M. Smith; 1988-274.

Chisels and Gouges

C hisels and gouges are among the most ancient tools used to shape wood, and their basic forms have remained the same for thousands of years. Despite their apparent simplicity, woodworkers needed them in a variety of sizes and shapes, each suited to a particular job. Eighteenth-century toolmakers accommodated these needs by producing a wide range of types for paring wood to size, shaping joints, cutting decorative designs, and shaping wood as it turned on a lathe.

While some eighteenth-century woodworking tools survive in large numbers, most types of chisels and gouges are comparatively rare. Few were made obsolete by changes in woodworking technology, so woodworkers continued to use them until, after thousands of sharpenings, they wore away to useless stubs.

English chisels and gouges often are stamped with the name of a manufacturer. In some cases, the name is that of the actual maker of the tool. In other cases, however, it is the name of a manufacturer who, in addition to selling his own products, bought and resold the work of others. For convenience in the descriptions of tools that follow, marks are usually taken to indicate their actual makers; in most instances, however, this assumption is open to question. Most chisel handles illustrated are old, but it is difficult to determine whether they are the original handles with which the blades were fitted when new.

TANGED CHISELS

Most chisels have flat blades. The types commonly used for general-purpose chopping and paring were called paring and firmer chisels (the latter of stronger construction) and were made with the back-end of the blade forged into a tapering pin or tang. Like most eighteenth-century chisels, these normally were sold as blades only. The woodworker fashioned a handle of the shape he desired, usually a tapering octagon, and drilled a hole in it so that it would fit tightly over the tang. An octagonal shoulder or bolster prevented the handle from sliding forward as the tool was pushed by hand or struck with a mallet.

Eighteenth-century English tanged chisels were made in a variety of sizes, up to at least 2 1/2 inches wide, and in different lengths and weights, but there is no evidence that they were made with beveled sides like modern paring chisels. Instead, their blades usually tapered to very thin edges, allowing them to be used to chop out dovetails and work in other tight locations.

The blade shapes of these chisels changed during the eighteenth and early nineteenth centuries. Until about 1750 or 1760, blades often flared in a continuous sweep like the English or Dutch example on the left, marked WILLIAM or WILLEM MOSES. The use of this design in England may have been a reflection of continuing Continental influences. By about 1770, the standard English shape was that of the second chisel, marked IOHN GREEN and made in Sheffield. It has a well-defined shank and slightly flaring blade. Shortly after 1800, blades became essentially parallel throughout their length, like that of the middle chisel by T. Shaw (probably Thomas Shaw of Bridgehouses near Sheffield, working 1787–1821). These chisels did not change in width as they were sharpened away. Over the next several decades the curve of the

shank became more abrupt as illustrated in the two right-hand chisels, both of which bear the mark of James Cam of Sheffield. The chisel on the far right also is stamped MARSHES & SHEPHERD, a mid-nineteenth-century Sheffield firm that acquired the right to use the Cam mark. Center chisel OL: 13". Top chisel by Thomas Newbould, ca. 1772, 1957-123, A8; left to right: 1992-205; courtesy of Edward Ingraham; 1992-185; private collection; private collection.

10

SOCKET CHISELS

Tanged chisels could not withstand heavy
beating, so heavy-duty chisels for work undertaken by carpenters, millwrights, and wheelwrights were made with the back-ends of their
blades forged as sockets. Their handles fit into
the sockets, and driving them with a mallet or
hammer only served to seat the handles more
firmly. Socket chisels made before the mid-
eighteenth century typically have six-sided sockets like the one by Samuel Freeth of Birmingham (left); they are found at early archaeological sites throughout Virginia. The origin of this
design is not known, but it may be Continental
since some German hunting spears and French
and German axes have faceted sockets. Unlike
the thinner, tanged chisels, the thick blades of
hexagonal-socket chisels often had beveled side
edges, allowing them to work more easily into
corners and other close spaces. During the
second half of the eighteenth century, possibly
as a result of the shift of chisel manufacture from
Birmingham to Sheffield, the elegant hexagonal-socket chisel gave way to a design with a
simple, tapering, round socket like that of the
chisel marked IOHN GREEN. It was much easier to
manufacture and fit with a handle. There were
at least two families of Greens making edge tools
in Sheffield. The IOHN GREEN mark probably
was used by those working in Burgess Street —
John Green & Son (ca. 1774), Hannah Green &
Son (ca. 1787), and John Green (1797–1821).
Freeth chisel OL: 13 1/8". Both handles are
replacements. Freeth chisel, 9078-O.C.; Green
chisel, 1982-245.

11

GOUGES

Gouges also were made in both tanged and socketed styles. Their blades were curved from side to side. Those with the sharpening bevel on the inside of the blade, like the left-hand gouge, were punched straight into the wood to produce a cut matching the outside curve of the blade. Those with the sharpening bevel on the outside were pushed into the wood at an angle to make hollowing cuts such as those required to fashion bowls and other scooped-out shapes. The first and fourth gouges bear the mark of the Sheffield firm of Philip Law (1773–1856); the second of Thomas Newbould (1773–1774), whose successors, Samuel Newbould (1787–1797) and Samuel Newbould & Company, were in busi-

ness into the twentieth century; and the third of William Weldon (1774–1787) or his successors, who were in operation until the mid-nineteenth century. As the dates indicate, these tools illustrate the problem of determining when Sheffield tools were made based on makers' marks. Some makers continued production well into the nineteenth century, while others, like James Cam and William Weldon, transferred the rights to use their marks to nineteenth-century successors. Law gouge OL: 12 1/8". Left to right: 1991-92; 1957-123, A7; courtesy of the Framingham Historical and Natural History Society, Framingham, Mass.; 1987-772.

MORTISE CHISELS

Mortise chisels cut the slots for mortise-and-tenon joints. Since the slot was made by pounding the chisel straight into the wood and then levering out the resulting chips, these chisels cut a slot whose width matched that of their blades. Accordingly, they were made in a range of sizes, and a woodworker needed several if he wished to make different size joints. Although only tanged types are shown here, they were made as socket chisels as well. Mortise chisels often received much less use than other types, and surviving early examples are relatively common.

The "clearance" angles on the blades of these tools provide an insight into the precision with which many early tools were made. The blades had to taper from their edges to their backs so that they would not stick in the work. Ground by eye, the dimensions of these angled surfaces and their tapers often are consistent to within several thousandths of an inch.

These Sheffield-made chisels are marked IOHN GREEN and date to the late eighteenth or early nineteenth centuries. Left-hand chisel OL: 11 3/8". Left to right: G1986-268, 70 and 71, gift of Frank M. Smith; 1985-102, 5; 1987-754.

13

MORTISE CHISEL BLADES

Like other chisel types, mortise chisel shapes evolved during the eighteenth century. The top example, by Sampson or Samuel Freeth of Birmingham, probably dates to the mid-eighteenth century or before. It has a blade that tapers toward its bolster. The chisel by Robert Moore, also of Birmingham, is probably somewhat later (although still pre-1775) and has a blade with a parallel top and bottom. Some early (ca. 1750–1770) Sheffield chisels also have parallel blades, but the standard late eighteenth- and nineteenth-century shape is that of the bottom three examples. Their blades taper toward the cutting edge.

These chisels also illustrate a general trend in makers' marks found on edge tools. Although there are exceptions, early Birmingham tools often have their maker's name embossed within a sunken rectangle. Sheffield marks of the third quarter of the century usually consist of large Roman letters struck into the iron (names are at times accompanied by devices such as crowns). Later Sheffield marks typically are of the same style, but smaller, although during the early nineteenth century some makers' names were embossed within a serrated border. Top to bottom: 1990-238; 1989-284; G1986-268, 68, gift of Frank M. Smith; 1989-267; 1990-239.

14

OTHER CHISEL TYPES

Chisels such as this heavy tanged chisel by Philip Law; the long, socketed mortise chisel marked WELDON; the V-shaped chisel, called a "bruzz" and used to shape mortises for wheel spokes, by one of the Mitchell firms; the turning chisel marked IOHN GREEN; and the oddly shaped gouge also by Green are a small sampling of the types produced for specialized tasks. All were made in Sheffield in the late eighteenth or early nineteenth century. The various Mitchell companies are documented 1797–1845. Mortising chisel OL: 22 3/4". Left to right: 1987-771; 1990-158; 1991-111; 1984-197; 1989-295.

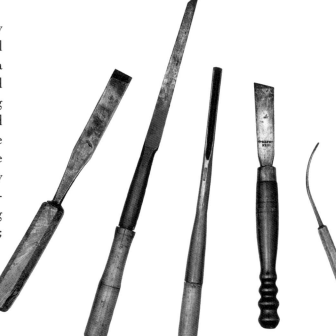

15

MANUFACTURING DETAILS

Despite the relatively low cost of English labor, toolmakers sought to use it to best advantage. As the marks around the tang of this Thomas Newbould chisel indicate, the use of dies made its forging easier and quicker. Careful attention generally was paid to the mechanical quality of tools, and their functional surfaces were shaped and finished to a fineness based upon the precision required of the tool. However, many tools illustrate that other, non-functional finishing operations frequently were executed with less concern for detail. The bolsters of most tanged chisels, for example, were coarsely and quickly filed to final shape with no attempt to polish out marks left by the file. 1957-123, A8.

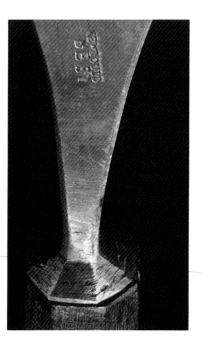

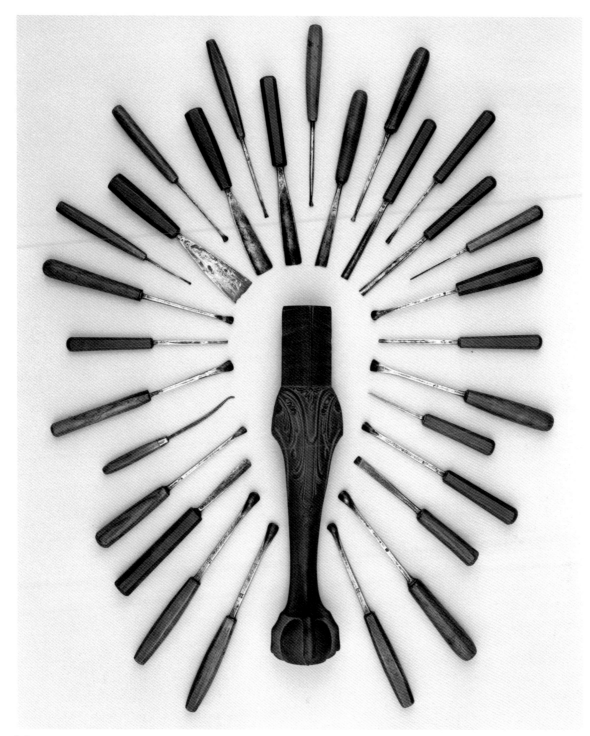

16

CARVING TOOLS

Carving tools, both chisel forms and gouges, were produced in an array of shapes and sizes suiting them to make different shaped cuts and to work in locations where normal chisels and gouges would not reach. Although carving tools had been made in many different designs for sculptors and carvers for centuries, commercial production during the eighteenth century made them readily available to the average cabinetmaker and architectural carver. This rare group of tools, probably dating to the last quarter of the century, is part of the tool kit brought to America by George William Cartwright II in 1819. Most are 8" to 10" long. G1986-268, gift of Frank M. Smith.

17

STEELING

The cutting edges of most edge tools were made of steel, a material consisting of iron and small amounts of carbon that can be hardened to the desired degree by controlled heating and cooling. Wrought iron, the material commonly used by blacksmiths, contains too little carbon to be hardened and is too soft to hold an effective edge. Cast iron, the direct product of blast furnaces, contains so much carbon that it is too brittle for edge tool manufacture.

The cost of raw materials was a significant portion of the total cost of making many tools, so toolmakers developed techniques that economized on materials whenever possible. Steel was readily available during the eighteenth century, but the processes involved in its manufacture made it more expensive than iron. As a result, most eighteenth-century edge tools were made principally of wrought iron with a small piece of steel welded onto their working edge as seen on this mortise chisel blade marked IOHN GREEN. The process was more labor-intensive than making the entire tool of steel, but the savings in material costs warranted the procedure. If repeated sharpenings wore away the steeled portion of the blade, the tool became useless unless it was resteeled. 1982-244, 2.

18

CAST STEEL

One of the most important improvements in edge tools during the eighteenth century was the introduction of better steel for their construction. For most of the century, cutting edges of tools were made either of German steel or blister steel. German steel, imported into England through Germany, was made directly from cast iron by reducing its carbon content. Blister steel was made by heating wrought iron embedded in charcoal so that the surface of the iron absorbed carbon. The resulting product had a blistered appearance. To produce a more homogeneous material, steelmakers cut blister steel apart and forge-welded it back together to mix high- and low-carbon portions. This was called shear steel. While German, blister, and shear steels had many desirable characteristics, they still were of inconsistent composition. During the late eighteenth century, Sheffield makers began to use cast steel, which was created by melting blister steel in crucibles so that it became a uniform liquid. The liquid steel was then cast into ingots from which the tools were forged. Using the new steel significantly improved the quality of edge tools.

Based upon surviving tools and the 1791 and 1793 stock inventories of London tool dealer Christopher Gabriel, it appears that carving tools, lightweight chisels and gouges, and saws were the first woodworking tools made of cast steel.[46] They probably were made entirely of the new material rather than of iron with an attached steel edge. Many of the Cartwright carving tools are stamped with a CS, indicating they were made of cast steel. Later tools made of cast steel often were stamped CAST STEEL, but no tools known with certainty to date before 1800 are so marked. G1986-268, 87, gift of Frank M. Smith.

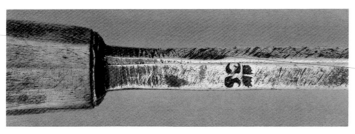

BLACKSMITH-MADE CHISELS AND GOUGES

While early American woodworkers imported most of their chisels and gouges, production of the simpler types was well within the capabilities of many American blacksmiths. Large numbers of blacksmith-made chisels survive, but since they normally were not marked and their designs are generic, distinguishing eighteenth-century examples from those produced later is virtually impossible. Turning gouge, chisel made from a file, and gouge with solid iron shank. Chisel OL: 7 1/2". W36-2333, Stephen C. Wolcott Collection; courtesy of Martyl and Emil Pollak; W36-637, Stephen C. Wolcott Collection.

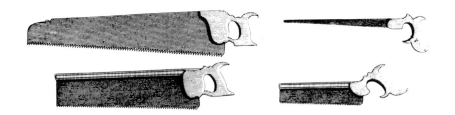

Saws

Of all hand tools used by eighteenth-century woodworkers, saws were among the most technically complex to manufacture. To work well, saw blades had to have a delicate balance between hardness so that they would stay sharp, stiffness so that they could be pushed through the work, flexibility so that they would bend rather than break under stress, and smoothness of surface so that they would not bind in the cut. Producing sheet steel for blades required either heavy forges or rolling mills. Hardening, tempering, straightening, and grinding the blades required great skill and water-powered grinding facilities. Often each manufacturing operation was the work of a different highly specialized toolmaker. With the exception of several late eighteenth-century manufacturers who produced heavy saws for use in sawmills, few Americans attempted to make saws before the nineteenth century; no documented eighteenth-century American-made saws are known.

Saws were made in many different types for work that ranged from sawing trees into logs to reducing boards to furniture parts to making the minute cuts of decorative piercings on musical instruments. Saws differed not only in size but also in the shapes and thicknesses of their blades, the design of their cutting teeth, and the style of their handles. English saws were of three basic types. Open saws were made of panels of steel with a handle at one or both ends (see Nos. 20 and 23). Backsaws also were made of steel panels, but since they were intended for finer work such as cutting joints, their blades were thin. To strengthen them, an iron or brass reinforcing rib was fitted over their backs, hence the name (see No. 24). Framed saws consisted of blades stretched between the ends of wooden or iron frames. This design allowed the use of narrower or thinner blades which, had they not been frame-mounted, would have been too flexible for use (see Nos. 26 and 27).

Like other tools that never became obsolete, eighteenth-century saws are quite rare. Only a dozen or so English examples that can be documented are known to survive.

20

CROSSCUT SAW

Crosscut saws were used by two sawyers, one on each end, who alternately pulled the saw to and fro. They were used for coarse work such as felling trees and sawing logs and heavy beams to length. This one was made by Thomas Barnard, who worked in Birmingham from about 1777 to 1797. OL: 4' 9". Courtesy of Malcolm MacGregor.

21

PITSAWS

Logs were sawn into boards using pitsaws. The log was raised on tall, sawhorse-like trestles or set over a pit. The top sawyer stood on the log and guided the saw along a line marked by snapping a string coated with chalk or charcoal. The pit man stood under the log, time after time pulling the saw down on its cutting stroke and helping to lift it back for the next pass. Pitsaws were made in both open "whipsaw" and framed types. The open saw on the right is 9' 1" long and is from Blandfield plantation in Essex County, Virginia. While we do not know if this is one of them, the plantation's owner, Robert Beverley, ordered "2 Whip saws for sawing a Pitt" from London in 1763.[47] The blade of the saw on the left, made by Samuel Newbould of Sheffield probably during the early nineteenth century, is stretched within a 7' 3 1/2" spruce frame, which is likely also of English origin. Similar framed saws, but with narrower blades, were used to saw out heavy curved timbers for constructing ships, buildings, and vehicles.

Despite the common use of water-powered sawmills on the Continent by at least the sixteenth century, the English continued to use pitsaws to cut logs into boards throughout the eighteenth century. Sawyers were numerous, they resisted the introduction of powered machinery, and there was little economic incentive to build mills. The situation in the American colonies was different. Good waterpower was available in many regions, wood was abundant and used more extensively as the primary building material, and, because of its relative scarcity, labor was more expensive. As a result, colo-

nists began to build sawmills shortly after settlement, and handsawing lumber was never as prevalent in America as in England. Nevertheless, American carpenters continued to use pitsaws to cut lumber on building sites, shipwrights used them to cut their heavy timbers, and woodworkers of other trades used them to saw boards of expensive wood (handsawing resulted in less waste) and to saw specially shaped pieces that were either impossible or inconvenient to obtain from mills. Blandfield saw, L1983-47, loaned by William Bradshaw Beverley; framed saw courtesy of Hank Allen.

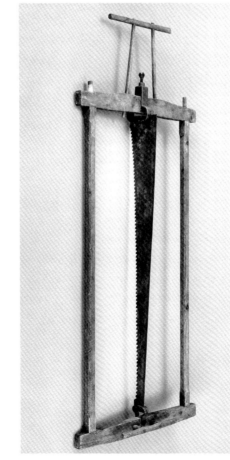

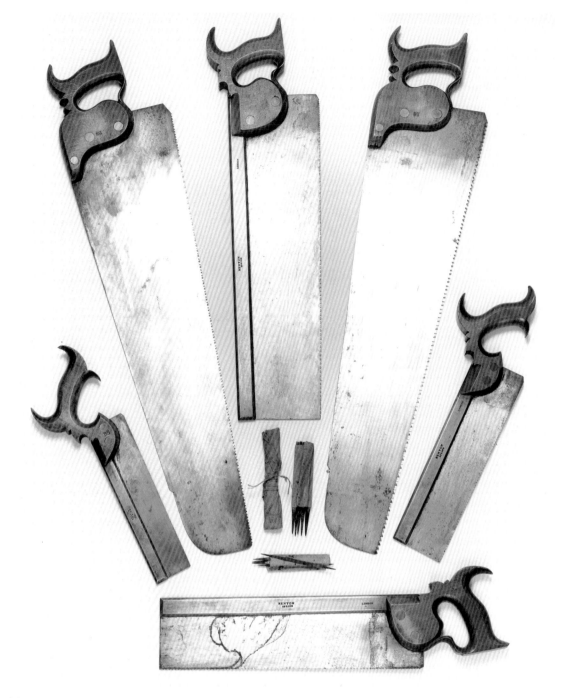

22

HANDSAWS AND BACKSAWS

Many Continental cabinetmakers, carpenters, and other woodworkers used framed saws to saw parts to shape and to cut joints. For most straight cuts, however, English and American woodworkers preferred open saws. These saws from the Benjamin Seaton chest were made by John Kenyon of Sheffield and were purchased in 1796 from the London planemaker and tool merchant Christopher Gabriel and Sons. They illustrate the types most commonly used. The two large saws are a handsaw (right, with coarser teeth) and a panel saw (left). Saws of similar design were made in a range of sizes, each with a different name. The largest, rip saws, had relatively coarse teeth designed for cutting along the grain of the wood. Smaller sizes, including handsaws and panel saws, had smaller teeth of a different design intended for finer cuts.

The other saws are backsaws, used primarily to cut joints. From smallest to largest, they are a dovetail saw, a carcass saw (the outside cases of chests-of-drawers, desks, and similar pieces of furniture were called "carcasses"), a sash saw (originally for making window sash), and a tenon saw. The smaller the saw, the finer were its teeth. This range of distinctly defined backsaws of different sizes probably was an eighteenth-century development brought about by the widespread need for tools for work ranging from fine to coarse. Although such saws probably were made in an assortment of sizes during the seventeenth century, documents lump them together simply as "tennant" saws.

The design details of these saws are typical of late century types. The hand- and panel saws have wide blades with straight backs and rounded noses. Their handles fully enclose the user's fingers and have flat bottoms. The backsaws have blades of nearly parallel width (there is some taper toward the front; other backsaws of this period have more). While the larger backsaws have closed handles, the smaller types have open, "dolphin-tail" grips. The small parcels are saw-sharpening files in their original paper wrappers. The hand- and panel saws have 26-inch blades. Courtesy of The Guildhall Museum, Rochester, Kent, Eng.; photography by John Melville.

23

EARLY HANDSAWS

Few English handsaws made before the late years of the century survive. These may be two of the earliest. The top saw has an illegible maker's mark and its handle is a replacement. The bottom saw, broken about halfway along its blade, was made by William Smith (1718–1750) of Birmingham and used by Judah Woodruff to build a meetinghouse and residences in Farmington, Connecticut, during the second half of the century. Note how the designs of the blade end of the top saw and the handle of the Wood-

ruff saw differ from the later Seaton saws (see No. 22). While the blades of these saws probably were forged using water-powered hammers, and some early saws had iron rather than steel blades, those dating from late in the century were likely to be made from rolled steel of much more consistent dimension and quality. OL: 23 1/2" and 16 3/4". Top, courtesy of Philip Walker; bottom, courtesy of the Stanley-Whitman House, Farmington, Conn., 417d.

24

MID-CENTURY TENON SAW

This tenon saw, also used by Judah Woodruff, is one of the earliest English backsaws
known. It was made by a maker named White,
about whom we know nothing except that during the mid-eighteenth century Virginians frequently ordered his saws by name because they
were considered to be of the highest quality.
The decorative filing at the front of the saw's
reinforcing back, the round-shaped front of the
handle, and the position of the handle on the
blade (mounted near the center of its back-end
rather than at the top) are all details that changed
over the course of the century. OL: 23 1/4".
Courtesy of the Stanley-Whitman House,
Farmington, Conn., 417c.

25

COMPASS SAW

Compass saws like this one made by James
Kenyon, John Kenyon, or Kenyon, Sykes &
Company of Sheffield about 1800 had long,
narrow, tapering blades so they could be insert-
ed into a drilled hole to make cuts in the center
of a board. Their narrow blades suited them for
sawing curved, or "compassed," shapes. OL:
13". Courtesy of Martyl and Emil Pollak.

26

FRAMED SAWS

The narrow blades of framed saws suited them for special tasks. The bow saw (below) had its blade mounted on the bottom of the frame and its tension was adjusted by twisting the cord on the top. Turning the handles changed the position of the blade in relation to the frame. It was used to saw curved work. Saws with blades mounted in the middle of the frame (right) were made in a variety of designs and sizes. Wheelwrights used them to saw the curved segments of wheel rims, and carpenters, cabinetmakers, and boat builders used them to saw curved parts such as chair legs and arms, parts of arches, and boat-framing members. Similar saws with narrow frames and wide, thin blades were used to resaw boards or saw veneers. Frames for such saws usually were homemade, and therefore they are difficult to date. The beech and pine bow saw is from the Cartwright tool kit and probably was made about 1800 or slightly before. The red oak, white pine, beech, and hickory saw probably was made by Samuel Wing of Sandwich, Massachusetts, between 1795 and 1815. OL: 26 1/2" and 48 1/4". Turning saw, G1986-268, 67, gift of Frank M. Smith; Samuel Wing saw courtesy of Old Sturbridge Village, Sturbridge, Mass., 86.17.3SW.

Pictorial Essay of Woodworking Tools

85

27

"MORRIS" SAW

Small framed saws for precise work often had metal frames and were made commercially. Although this saw may be Continental, it is similar to "Morris" saw frames that are illustrated in the eighteenth-century tool catalog of John Wyke of Liverpool. Both wood- and metalworkers used Morris saws. OL: 14". Courtesy of Gene W. Kijowski.

28

SAW MARKINGS

One of the primary distinctions between edge tools of different qualities was the steel from which they were made. In the 1790s, Christopher Gabriel of London sold saws made of German steel, cast steel, and "London Spring" steel. Backsaws were available with either iron or brass reinforcing backs. About 1800, sawmakers began to mark their products with the steel from which they were made. The marks illustrated are on backsaws made between about 1790 and 1820. Top to bottom: John Kenyon, Sheffield, 1991-460; William Moorman, London, 1990-257; John Spear, Sheffield, 1990-182.

Many saws made shortly after 1800 have three crowns stamped to the side and above their maker's name. The significance of the crowns is unknown, although one writer has noted they might be a mark of quality.[48] This mark is on a handsaw by John Kenyon or Kenyon, Sykes & Company of Sheffield. Courtesy of Edward Ingraham.

SAW SHARPENING TOOLS

Woodworkers owned a variety of sharpening stones and other implements for maintaining their tools. Saw teeth were sharpened using files, and the teeth were bent slightly outward in an alternating pattern using a tool known as a wrest. "Setting" the teeth this way resulted in a saw that made a cut slightly wider than the thickness of its blade, allowing it to move more freely in the cut and permitting the user to guide the saw more accurately. The backsaw is shown with a triangular file and a small wrest of the types used to sharpen and set back- and handsaws. The half-round frame- or pitsaw file and heavy-duty wrest are alongside a pitsaw whose original tooth pattern (teeth to the left) has been modified by repeated sharpenings (teeth to the right). Large saw set OL: 9 5/8". Triangular saw file by P. S. Stubs, Warrington, England, early nineteenth century; small wrest, probably Birmingham and late eighteenth or early nineteenth century; frame-saw file, marked DUBLIN, probably Sheffield, ca. 1772; large wrest, possibly American, found in a Williamsburg house in the early 1950s; backsaw with illegible mark, England, mid- to late eighteenth century; pitsaw, England, probably nineteenth century. Courtesy of the Paul B. Kebabian Collection; 1992-114; 1957-123, A11; 1953-267; G1986-268, 66, gift of Frank M. Smith; W36-1944, Stephen C. Wolcott Collection.

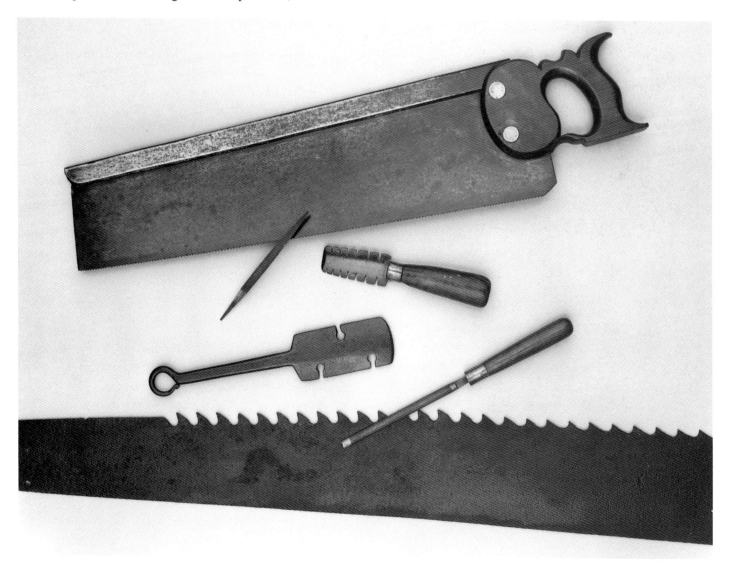

Pictorial Essay of Woodworking Tools

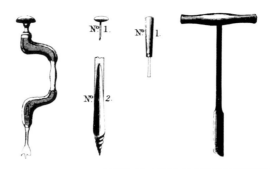

Tools for Boring Holes

Many wooden products required that their makers bore holes for assembling parts. The holes ranged from the tiny mounts for harpsichord jack springs — made of hog bristles — to four- or five-inch holes bored through logs to make pumps and water pipes. Musical instrument makers and cabinetmakers drilled holes through instrument soundboards, chair splats, and galleries to begin the cuts for sound holes and pierced frets and strapwork. Carpenters, shipwrights, and millwrights bored holes to clear much of the waste from large mortises for mortise-and-tenon joints and to create holes for the pins, pegs, and bolts that held their products together. The blunt-ended woodscrews used during the eighteenth century required pilot holes, and unless forged nails were driven into pre-drilled holes, they tended to split the wood they were intended to hold together. Many of these holes were not simply straight. Spinning wheel parts, wagon wheels and their axles, and barrel bungs, or stoppers, and spigots were fitted using tapered holes. The heads of wooden screws often were seated into tapered holes so that they were flush with the surface around them.

Woodworkers used many different styles and sizes of tools to bore these holes. Many, such as the huge tapered reamers used to shape holes in wheel hubs or smaller tapered bits with built-in stoppers for drilling holes to receive barrel spigots, were highly specialized and designed for only one job. Others were general-purpose tools — augers for drilling large or deep holes, bits that fit into braces, and gimlets, which resembled miniature augers. Many boring tools in a range of types and sizes survive, but unlike chisels, saws, and planes, most of the earliest appearing do not bear makers' marks or survive with documented histories. It is therefore very difficult to determine which were made in the eighteenth century and which later.

30

NOSE AUGER

Augers were the common tools for boring large holes. Mid-eighteenth-century Virginia storekeepers sold them by one-quarter-inch increments, from one-quarter to two inches. With the exception of "screw" augers, eighteenth-century Virginia documents do not indicate the shape of the cutting blades of these tools, but most probably were like this one, a half-cylinder with a cutting lip or "nose" forged on its end. Turned intermittently using the long handle, these augers required that a small depression be made in the wood to guide the tool as it began its cut, and the auger had to be withdrawn from the hole periodically to remove the shavings that accumulated in its blade. Woodworkers usually bought only the blade and fitted it with a handle of their own manufacture.

The mark on this auger is that of Thomas Smith (1770–1788, 1800–1803) of Deritend near Birmingham. OL: 14 1/2", with a 3/4" cutting diameter. Courtesy of the Framingham Historical and Natural History Society, Framingham, Mass.

31

SCREW AUGER

Screw or spiral augers had several advantages. The small screw on the tool's end positioned the auger on the work and eliminated the need for a starting hole. As the artisan turned the auger, it drew itself into the work with little downward pressure and it automatically lifted the shavings from the hole. The first documentation for a spiral auger with a lead screw dates to the 1770s. Although they apparently were not commonly used until after numerous improvements were made by American toolmakers in the nineteenth century, "screw" augers occasionally appear in late eighteenth-century documents including Virginia woodworkers' estate inventories. This auger was made in Mansfield, Connecticut, by Ephraim and/or Lucius Gurley. The Gurleys made augers from at least 1814 through 1848. OL: 17 1/4", with a 2 1/4" cutting diameter. Courtesy of Old Sturbridge Village, Sturbridge, Mass., 2.121.133.

32

TAPERED REAMER

This huge reamer—its blade is thirty-three inches long—was made by D. Frank or Frant, a Pennsylvania blacksmith, probably during the late eighteenth or early nineteenth century. A hook, now broken, at the end of the reamer was used to draw the tool through the work. Wheelwrights used these tools to taper previously bored holes in wheel hubs to receive metal bearings for the axle. Some early American blacksmith-made tools with makers' marks survive, but unless the mark includes a maker's full name rather than only initials or a symbolic device, identifying him and the tool's date of manufacture is difficult. Courtesy of the collection of Byron B. Wenger.

33

GIMLETS

Gimlets are essentially miniature augers used to drill small holes, including those for starting nails and screws. The gimlets in this set, made by Thomas Smith of Deritend near Birmingham about 1772, are the typical eighteenth-century English type with a half-cylinder body and lead screws on their ends to draw them into the work. The smallest drills a hole of about one-eighth-inch diameter. They were sold fitted with boxwood handles turned on a lathe. The turner cut two thin lines at the middle of each handle to speed up the task of mounting the blades accurately. Largest OL: 5 1/8". 1957-123, A19-23.

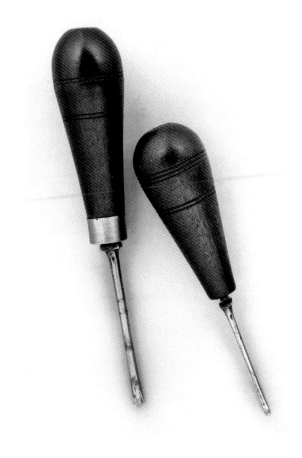

34

BRAD AWLS

Although brad awls look like small chisels or screwdrivers, they were tools used to bore pilot holes for nails and brads quickly. The blade of the awl was pushed and twisted into the wood so that it separated the fibers, leaving a hole. These brad awls were included in the 1773 Hewlett gentleman's tool chest. Their commercially made turned handles with decorative lines are a typical eighteenth-century type, but the cast-brass reinforcing ferrule and the use of mahogany for handles were elegant refinements. Ferrules on tool handles made before the late eighteenth century usually were iron, while commercially made English handles typically were beech, or, as in the case of the gimlets in No. 33, boxwood. Largest OL: 5 3/8". 1957-123, A12 and 13.

35

HOMEMADE BRACE

The brace, or bitstock, was known by at least the fifteenth century. The user held the tool's revolving top in one hand or against his chest and turned the crank with the other. This provided a continuous drilling motion. Some tradesmen who repeatedly drilled holes of the same size, including coopers who required holes to dowel together the boards forming the heads of their barrels or chairmakers who joined turned parts by inserting their ends into holes, used braces with permanently attached bits. Other woodworkers used braces with interchangeable bits. Many eighteenth-century woodworkers made their own braces. This example, produced by Nathaniel Dominy V at East Hampton on Long Island in 1802, is typical. Each bit is fitted into a wooden "pad" that slipped into the end of the bitstock. OL (excluding bit): 13 1/4". Courtesy, Winterthur Museum, 57.26.18.

36

FLAT-TANG BIT

The tangs or mounting ends of bits found at colonial Virginia archaeological sites usually are broad and flat. This design resisted the twisting forces that could cause bits to tear loose from their wooden pads. This center bit probably was made by Benjamin Freeth of Birmingham between the mid- eighteenth and early nineteenth century. OL: 4 5/8", cutting diameter 5/8". Collection of the Mercer Museum of the Bucks County Historical Society, Doylestown, Pa., 15228.

37

BRACES WITH IRON PADS

English toolmakers were producing iron chucks (also called "pads") for braces at least by the 1750s. They were much stronger than the chuck systems used on all-wooden braces, and since the bits fit directly into a socket in the end of the iron pad, there was no need for the woodworker to mount each bit individually into a wooden pad. These early metal pads were of two types. Some had thumbscrews that tightened against the bit tang. Others had internal springs that pressed a small catch into a notch filed into the bit. The spring catch was released by a push button on the side of the pad. Iron padmakers sold their products both to commercial bracemakers and, through retailers, to individual woodworkers. These pads, made by John Ryley of Birmingham between about 1770 and 1785, are mounted on (left) a homemade ash brace and (right) what is probably an early example of a commercially made brace of mahogany and boxwood. The thumbscrew is a replacement. OL: 14 5/8" and 14 3/4". 1991-99; 1991-154.

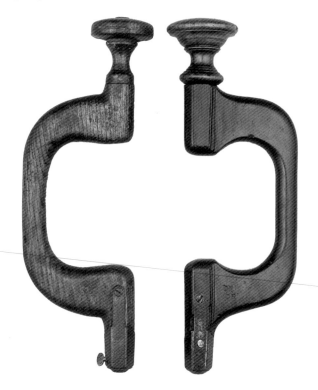

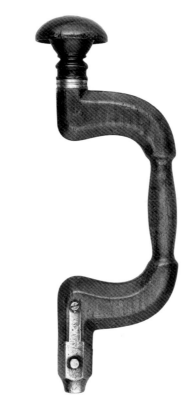

38

BRACE WITH BRASS PAD

Late eighteenth-century bracemakers continued to refine their products. They improved the mountings of the rotating heads and fitted braces with pads made of brass with an iron-lined socket for the bit. These cast-brass pads were more eye-catching, and probably were less expensive to fabricate and finish, than the forged iron type with their decorative moldings. This brace was sold by York planemaker John Green, although it is likely he bought it from a specialist bracemaker for resale. It was made before about 1810. OL: 13 3/4". 1989-408.

39

SQUARE-TANG BITS

The introduction of iron and brass pads required the redesign and standardization of bit tangs. The old flat style gave way to bits with square, tapering tangs. Those intended for use in push-button braces were filed with notches to receive the spring-mounted catch. Bits were made in a variety of designs for different jobs. By the 1760s, braces were sold with sets of bits, and standard late century sets consisted of up to thirty-six different styles and sizes. London planemaker George Mutter sold these bits before 1799. He probably obtained them from a Birmingham or Sheffield maker. They are (clockwise) shell bits, nose bits, a taper bit, and center bits. The bit mounted in the brace is a countersink for making depressions to receive the heads of wood screws. Taper bit OL: 5". Brace, 1989-408; bits, 1991-459, 30-38.

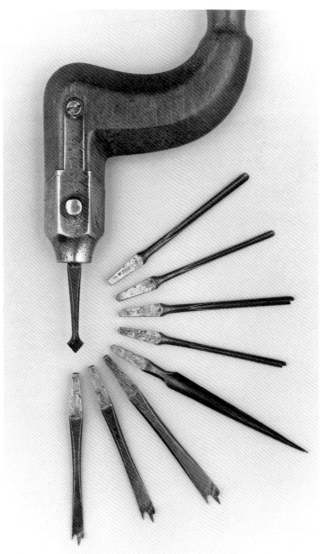

40

METAL BRACE

All-metal braces were made commercially and also by local blacksmiths. They were stronger than wooden braces and thus suited for heavy-duty use by wheelwrights and other artisans who drilled both wood and metal. This unmarked "cagehead" brace, so named because of the struts in its head, probably was made by an American blacksmith in the eighteenth or early nineteenth century. OL (excluding bit): 14 1/2". 1935-70.

41

BOW DRILL

Several types of drills were available for boring small holes. In the case of the bow drill, a string held taunt by a bow was wrapped around the drum of the drill. As the bow was pushed and pulled, the string turned the drill in a reciprocating motion. This drill has a built-in head for holding its upper end. The bow is marked HOOLE, and both it and the drill were made in the late eighteenth or early nineteenth century, probably in England. Drill (without bit) OL: 7 1/2". Courtesy of Donald and Anne Wing.

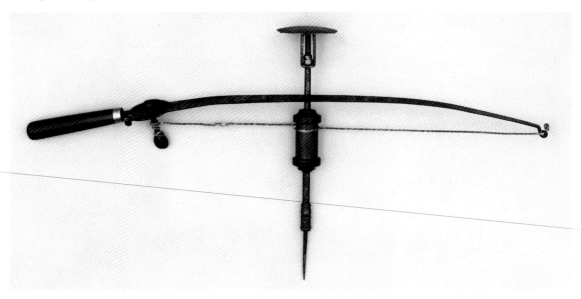

Tools: Working Wood in Eighteenth-Century America

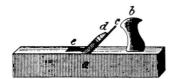

Planes

Planes were invented by the Romans, if not the Greeks before
them, and were used by almost all eighteenth-century woodworkers. Most eighteenth-century planes fall into three basic catego-
ries. Bench planes were used to reduce hewn, split, or sawn wood to
the final size needed, to make it consistently flat and straight or, in
some cases, curved, and to smooth its surfaces. Joining planes cut
grooves, steps, and other interlocking shapes so that parts could be
joined tightly and accurately. Molding planes cut decorative shapes.
In addition, there were planes designed for special tasks such as
shaping violin backs and bellies, rounding ships' spars, hollowing out
wooden gutters, and smoothing concave curves like the inside of
wheel rims. While many of these tasks could be performed with simple
edge tools like chisels and gouges, planes allowed the work to be done
with much greater speed and accuracy.

Many joining and molding planes were highly specialized tools
that made cuts of only one particular shape and size. As a result,
woodworkers needed a different plane for each shape they wanted to
produce. Virginia documents mention over thirty different types.
Artisans who made products with a variety of such shapes often
owned large numbers of planes, and between different types and sizes,
it was not uncommon for Virginia joiners' kits to include forty to
seventy. Some, like bench planes, were in constant use, and few have
survived. Others, like many joining and molding planes that were used
only occasionally, have survived in great numbers.

Planes have been of special interest to tool collectors because
many of their makers stamped their names on the planes' front
surfaces or toes. It is not known why this practice became so widespread among English and American planemakers when many other
tools remained unmarked. Those names, gathered from the toes of
thousands of planes, have served as a starting point for documentary
research about their makers. As a result, much more is known about
planemakers and the evolution of plane types than about any other
eighteenth-century toolmaking trade or its products.

42

PLANE PARTS AND NOMENCLATURE

Planes consist of a chisel-like blade, called the iron, which is mounted in a body or stock. The stock, usually made of wood during the eighteenth century, held the iron firmly at a preset angle and positioned it relative to the wood it was cutting. The extent to which the iron projected beyond the stock determined the depth of the cut made with each pass of the plane. In use, the plane was run over the wood a number of times, cutting a relatively thin shaving until the desired shape was produced. This mahogany jackplane was made about 1772, probably in London. 1957-123, A6.

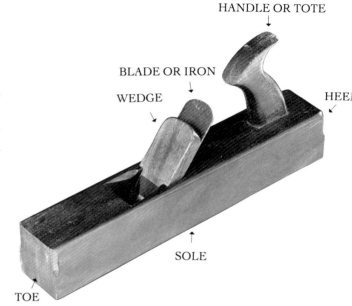

HANDLE OR TOTE

BLADE OR IRON

WEDGE

HEEL

SOLE

TOE

43

BENCH PLANES

The wooden parts of bench planes are relatively simple to make, and eighteenth-century woodworkers often made their own. Bench planes were also available from specialist planemakers, and these are among the earliest commercially produced, English examples known. The smallest and two largest planes were made by William Madox in London (1748–1775); the next to smallest was made by John Harris, an ironmonger and planemaker in Bath (documented 1777–1781, this plane probably ca. 1770). Woodworkers used these planes progressively to size and smooth boards.

The next to smallest was a jack or fore plane. Our understanding of the distinction between the two types during the eighteenth century is vague, but fore planes probably were somewhat longer than jacks. Jack planes were used to remove large amounts of wood quickly, and the convex edges of their blades produced the trough-shaped cuts often seen on drawer bottoms, furniture backs, and other roughly

planed pieces. (While jack planes could have either flat or slightly curved soles, the sole of this particular example is unusual because its curve is asymmetrical. Although of a jack plane form, it may have been intended for a special, specific purpose.) The two largest planes are a try plane (second from left) and a jointer (left). They were used to straighten and smooth lumber previously planed with the jack. Since longer planes tend to ride upon the "hills" of uneven stock, they shave those high areas level rather than following them up and down. The longer the plane, the more effective it is at this task. Jointers, the longest planes, were used most commonly to plane the edges of boards to be joined edge-to-edge. The smallest plane, a smoother, was used for final, very fine surfacing and smaller jobs where a longer plane would have been unnecessary or inconvenient. OL: 30", 22 1/8", 12 1/2", and 7 3/8". Left to right: 1992-197; G1986-268, 19, gift of Frank M. Smith; 1991-102; G1986-268, 26, gift of Frank M. Smith.

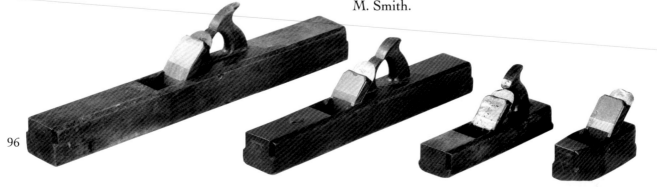

44

AMERICAN BENCH PLANES

A professionally made American jack plane by Cesar Chelor, Wrentham, Massachusetts, 1753–1784, and a homemade American smoother with carved initials IM and 1778. Both have irons by the Birmingham maker Robert Moore. OL: 14 1/4" and 8 3/8". Courtesy of the Paul B. Kebabian Collection and Edward Ingraham.

45

SINGLE AND DOUBLE IRONS

An important improvement in bench planes was the development of the "double" iron. First recorded in a 1767 advertisement of Philadelphia planemaker Samuel Caruthers, who undoubtedly imported the irons for his planes from England, it was almost certainly an English innovation. Earlier bench plane irons consisted only of a single blade (right). When planing wood with twisted or irregular grain, these irons often raised splinters ahead of the cut, which resulted in a rough surface. The double iron (left) had a "top iron" fitted to its blade. This top iron caused the shavings to curl away from the iron and break, preventing them from pulling up the wood before it was sheared by the cutting iron. Both are marked IOHN GREEN and were made in Sheffield during the late eighteenth century. OL: 6 1/2" and 6". G1986-268, 21 and 31, gift of Frank M. Smith.

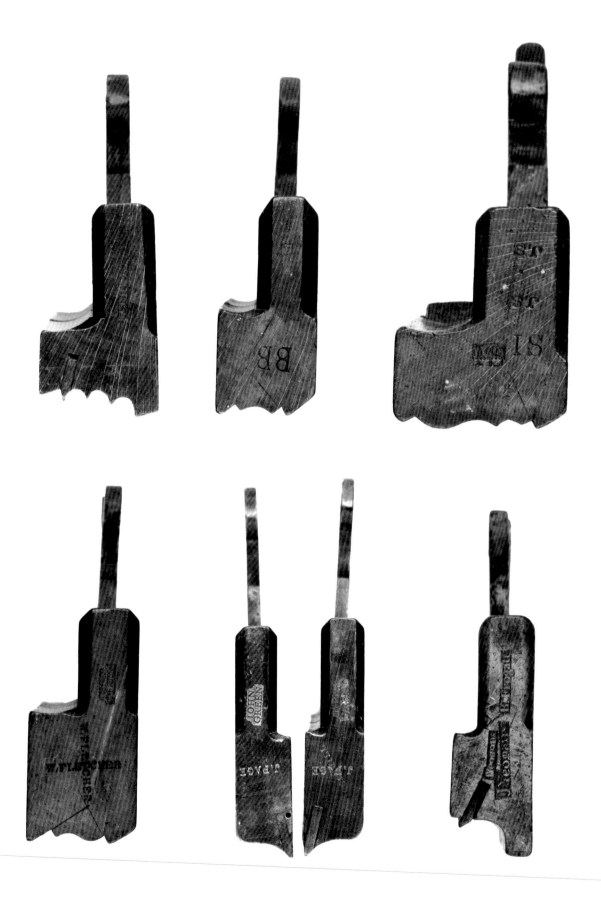

Tools: Working Wood in Eighteenth-Century America

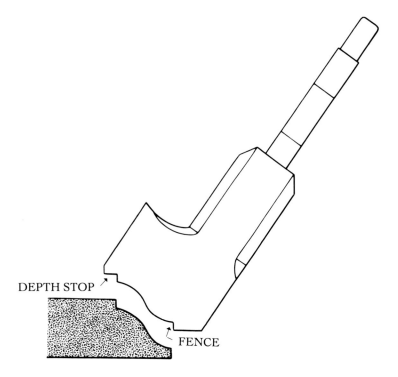

DEPTH STOP

FENCE

46

MOLDING PLANES

Molding planes cut shapes that were the reverse of their soles. This group of mid- to late eighteenth-century English planes shows only a tiny sampling of the molding plane shapes and sizes made. Note that each plane is stamped with its maker's mark on the upper portion of its toe (embossed vertical marks). The other stamped names are those of the planes' owners. English woodworkers stamped tools with their names much more frequently than Americans, possibly because their trade organizations insured tools against loss and required such identification to prove ownership. Information about English and American planemakers can be found in the books published by Goodman, Roberts, and Pollak included in the Further Reading. Left to right, top: reed plane, John Cogdell, London, 1750–1765; square ovolo, John Sym, London, 1753–1803; reverse ogee and astragal, John or Anna Jennion, London, 1732–1778; bottom: ogee, John Green, York, 1768–1808; pair of snipe bills, John Green, York, 1768–1808; bead, Benjamin Frogatt, Birmingham, 1760–1790. 1991-617; 1982-138; 1990-102; 1982-255; 1983-206, 1 and 2; 1990-107.

Like many eighteenth-century tools, molding planes appear to be very simple at first glance, but analyzing the details of their design and construction reveals that they were quite sophisticated. Thin strips of boxwood or other hard woods were incorporated into plane soles to reduce wear, especially at otherwise fragile points. The fence rode against the edge of the board being planed and positioned the tool properly. The depth stop caused the plane to stop cutting when the molding had been fully formed. The "spring" of the plane—the angle at which it was designed to be used—made it easier to hold the plane against the wood and improved the iron's cutting action. Although not shown here, planes were made with their irons set at different vertical angles relative to the plane sole. Common planes had their irons set between forty-five and fifty degrees; those for hardwoods were set higher so that the iron made more of a scraping cut, producing a finer finish on the harder material. Using such tools, woodworkers could produce long lengths of very precise moldings quickly and repeatedly.

47

HOLLOWS AND ROUNDS

While many molding planes were designed for making only one shape of cut, others were for more general-purpose shaping. Hollows and rounds cut corresponding round and hollow shapes. They were useful for shaping and smoothing curved surfaces and also could be used in combinations to produce the various curves of complex moldings for which the wood-worker did not have a specific plane. By the 1790s, hollows and rounds were made in sets of up to eighteen pairs. This set, consisting of twenty-eight of its original thirty-two planes, was made by Benjamin Dyson of York, England, in the late eighteenth century. Tool dealers began to offer other types of tools in sets of various sizes during the century. While many woodworkers continued to purchase individual tools as they needed them, this marketing technique almost certainly promoted sales among affluent customers. 1982-131, 1-28.

48

HOLLOW AND ROUND PAIR

A hollow and round pair, number "9," by Samuel Green (1774–1801) of Bristol, England. These planes were imported into America and owned by Thomas Nixon of Framingham, Massachusetts, during the late eighteenth century. Courtesy of the Framingham Historical and Natural History Society, Framingham, Mass.

ASSEMBLY MARKS

While the consistency of design and sureness of manufacture of surviving but unmarked seventeenth- and very early eighteenth-century molding planes suggest that they were made by toolmakers who produced them in quantity, woodworkers of that period often made their own. By the late seventeenth century, however, joiners and cabinetmakers needed a much larger variety of special purpose planes to make the diversity of shapes demanded by the elaborate woodwork coming into fashion. As the complexity of plane types and shapes and the numbers required increased, many woodworkers found it advantageous to purchase them from specialist makers who employed tools and techniques that permitted more efficient production. For example, specialists could produce similar planes in batches. The parts of this late

eighteenth-century cove and astragal molding plane by John Cox, Sr., of Birmingham are all numbered "16"—in pencil on the stock and wedge and in filed Roman numerals on the iron. The numbers allowed Cox to keep track of each plane's parts as he worked on the group. He no doubt filed the iron to the desired shape and marked it indelibly so that its number would not be removed when the iron was hardened by heat treating. Courtesy of Trip Kahn — Rockhill Research.

EVOLUTION OF MOLDING PLANE STYLES

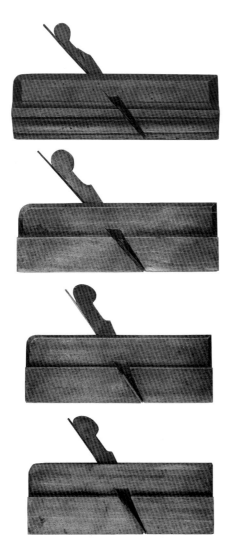

Over the course of the eighteenth century, the details of English plane design evolved in a definite pattern. These London-made tools illustrate the evolution of molding planes. Their overall length decreased from over ten inches at the beginning of the century to a standard nine and one-half inches by about 1770 and remained there throughout the nineteenth century. The details of individual makers' products varied, but generally, wedge finials changed from round to elliptical, and chamfers and other decorative touches became less bold and more highly standardized, probably as a result of efforts to speed production and market tools that conformed to generally accepted designs. While decorative, many features of planes such as chamfers and wedge finials were also utilitarian. Finials made the wedges easier to remove, and chamfers made the planes less likely to splinter and more comfortable to hold. Top to bottom: ovolo by Robert Wooding, ca. 1705, OL: 10 3/8"; number 16 hollow by John Cogdell, mid-eighteenth century; number 12 hollow by John Sym, late eighteenth century; number 12 hollow by John Lund, ca. 1820. 1986-34; 1982-223; 1991-619, 2; 1952-277, 49.

51

NEW ENGLAND PLANES

Planemakers were among the first documented American specialist toolmakers. The earliest known of a large group of New England makers was Francis Nicholson, who worked in Wrentham, Massachusetts, from about 1728 until 1753 (see Fig. 18). Other pre-Revolutionary New England makers included (across the top) Nicholson's son John (Wrentham, Massachusetts, probably working 1733–1763), John Walton, Jr. (Reading, Massachusetts, b. 1710–d. 1785), and Henry Wetherel (Norton, Massachusetts, pre-1780) as well as (center, top to bottom) Nathaniel Briggs (Norton, Massachusetts, and Keene, New Hampshire, b. 1744–d. 1777), Samuel Doggett (Dedham, Massachusetts, b. 1727–d. 1794), and A. Hide (possibly Asa Hide of Norwich, Connecticut, pre-1780). The number of planemakers working in southeastern New England increased during the late eighteenth century. While generally following English designs, their planes are recognizable as American products because of their often distinct detailing and the fact that they usually were made of yellow birch rather than beech, the preferred wood of English makers. The length of New England molding planes did not become standardized to nine and one-half inches until after 1800. Nicholson cornice plane, W36-2047, Stephen C. Wolcott Collection; Doggett molding plane, 1991-562; remainder courtesy of Martyl and Emil Pollak.

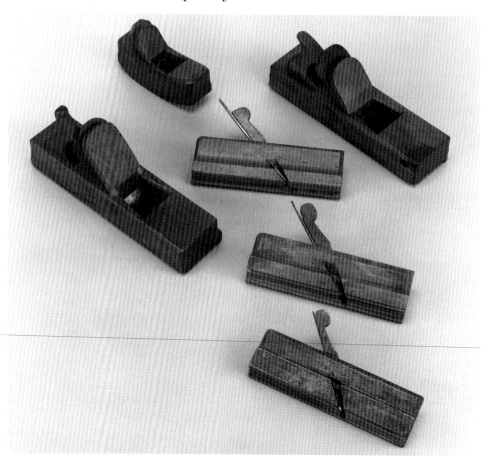

PLANES MADE BY CESAR CHELOR

Cesar Chelor, the slave of Francis Nichol-son, was one of the earliest professional American planemakers. In his 1753 will, Nicholson freed Chelor and bequeathed him tools and timber. Chelor continued to make planes until his death in 1784. The top plane was used to form raised panels. The molding plane cuts a reverse ogee and astragal. OL: 12 7/8" and 10". Courtesy of Martyl and Emil Pollak.

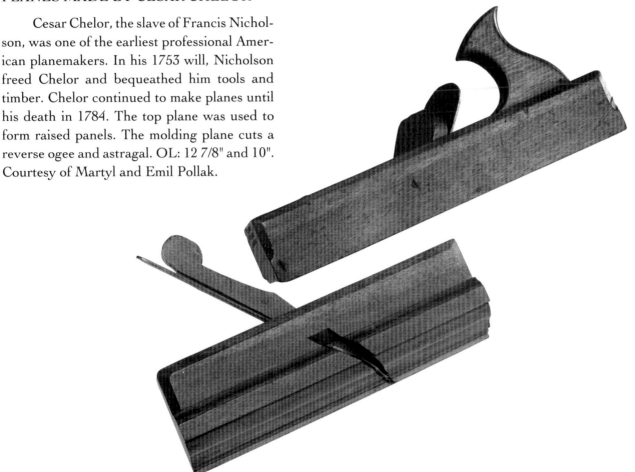

JOINING PLANES

Many joining planes were variations on the rabbet plane, a tool designed to create steps and grooves. While a variety of joints could be created using simple rabbet planes or even saws and chisels, specialized planes such as the moving fillister and dado, developed during the eighteenth century, had either fixed or adjustable fences and depth stops that made them more efficient tools. These planes speeded up the work they performed and reduced the skill required of their users. Rabbet plane by Benjamin Frogatt, Birmingham, England, 1760–1790; fillister, unmarked, England, ca. 1770; moving fillister by Benjamin Frogatt, Birmingham, England, 1760–1790, all from the Nixon tool kit. Courtesy of the Framingham Historical and Natural History Society, Framingham, Mass. Tongue and groove planes by the Stotherts of Bath, England, early nineteenth century. Courtesy of Martyl and Emil Pollak. Stothert planes are known to have been imported to America. Dado plane by John Sym, London, ca. 1775, brought to New York by George W. Cartwright II in 1819. G1986-268, 12, gift of Frank M. Smith.

RABBET

FILLISTER

MOVING FILLISTER

TONGUE AND GROOVE

DADO

ENGLISH PLOW

Plow planes were used to cut grooves, frequently in the edges of boards to receive panels, as in doors. In use since at least the sixteenth century, they were among the most complex planes, with adjustable fences that determined the groove's distance from the edge of the board, an adjustable depth stop that determined the groove's depth, and sets of interchangeable blades whose width determined the groove's width. This plow was made by John Cogdell in London in the mid-eighteenth century; the irons were made in Sheffield by Philip Law in the late eighteenth or early nineteenth century. Plow stock OL: 7 1/2". Plow iron widths run by sixteenths from one-eighth to nine-sixteenths inch. 1991-620; 1983-332, 1-8.

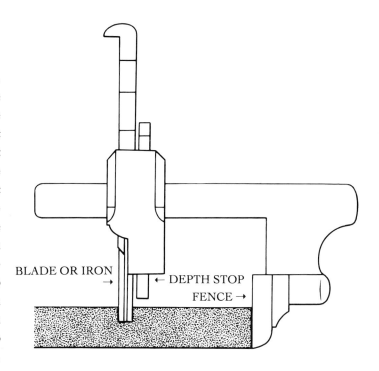

BLADE OR IRON →   ← DEPTH STOP   FENCE →

55

YANKEE PLOW

New England plows developed along somewhat different lines than their English counterparts. The "Yankee" plow was longer and the arms that supported its fence often were secured with wooden screws, an improvement over the English system of fixing the fence with wedges. This plow probably was made in the late eighteenth or early nineteenth century by Thomas Nixon of Framingham, Massachusetts, for his own use. Stock OL: 9 15/16". Courtesy of the Framingham Historical and Natural History Society, Framingham, Mass.

POST-REVOLUTIONARY AMERICAN PLANES

Specialist planemakers also worked in Pennsylvania and other regions outside of New England before the Revolution. During the late eighteenth century, their numbers grew, especially in urban areas. Planes such as (clockwise from left) this molding plane by Jeremiah and John Douglass (ca. 1796) of New York, plow by William Brooks (1791–1807) of Philadelphia, panel raiser by Dietrich Heis (b. 1745–d. 1819) of Lancaster, Pennsylvania, and molding plane by William Vance (1799–1833) of Baltimore tended to adhere closely to English models, including the use of beech for their stocks. In contrast to the British, however, nineteenth-century American makers usually made their plows with threaded arms; their fences were locked into position by wooden nuts. Douglass, Brooks, and Heis planes courtesy of Martyl and Emil Pollak; Vance plane, used by Andrew Hack of Baltimore, G1992-64, 49, gift of T. Ridgeway Trimble.

57

SASH PLANES

Many developments in plane design may have been introduced by planemakers seeking to increase sales of their products. Other developments were the result of changing consumer demands, just as refinements of saws and the large-scale production of carving tools were prompted by a market for more finely made and decorated furniture and architectural interiors. Consumer demand for more elegant drop-leaf tables resulted in the production of planes to make the curved "rule" joints (named because they resemble the joints of folding rules) that supported the raised leaf along its entire length and hid the opening between the leaf and the top when the leaf was down.

Beginning about 1700, the newly introduced wooden double-hung sash window prompted tool developments that continued through the century. Among the new tools were sash planes of various types to cut the moldings and grooves for the glass on window mullion bars. While the English preferred separate planes for these operations (left), American planemakers frequently made combination planes, called stick-and-rabbet planes, that cut the molding and groove simultaneously. Sash fillister, W. Squire, England (ca. 1760); sash ovolo, John Cogdell, London (1750–1765); sash plane, Samuel Dean, Dedham, Massachusetts (mid- to late eighteenth century); and adjustable "stick-and-rabbet" plane, John or George Butler, Philadelphia (1791–1835). 1992-117; 1982-224; latter two planes courtesy of Martyl and Emil Pollak.

ROMAN AND GRECIAN MOLDINGS

Other tools changed more subtly to meet changing consumer tastes. The shapes cut by molding planes were highly standardized based upon generally accepted notions of properly constructed classical decoration. Thus planes designed to cut a given shape (ogee, astragal, ovolo, etc.), whether by English or American makers, produced amazingly consistent forms. As molding designs based upon ancient Grecian prototypes became popular during the late eighteenth century, planemakers began to create planes that cut these designs, often derived geometrically from the ellipse (right), in addition to the more traditional ancient Roman types (left), usually based upon arcs of circles (or close approximations). Woodworkers without these new planes were at a disadvantage when their customers wanted the most up-to-date and fashionable products. The Roman ogee is by John Sym of London, ca. 1780. The nineteenth-century Grecian plane is by John Sleeper (d. 1834) of Newburyport, Massachusetts, and Chester, New Hampshire. 1982-254; courtesy of Martyl and Emil Pollak.

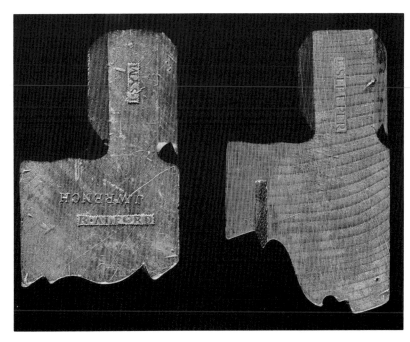

IMPROVED PLANES

Overall advances in English metalworking techniques during the late eighteenth century often improved both the function and the appearance of woodworking tools. The ready availability of brass castings, which could be produced and finished in large quantities more readily than similar pieces could be forged in iron, led to the wider use of ferrules to reinforce plane parts such as plow fence arm ends. Depth stops made of brass or brass and iron combinations replaced easily worn wooden types. They often were regulated with thumbscrews, a development made practical by the availability of efficiently manufactured machine screws. British makers also began to experiment with screws to adjust plow fences and other moving parts of tools such as the marking points of mortise gauges. Plow plane by the Gabriel firm of London and dado plane by John Green of York, England, both late eighteenth or early nineteenth century. Stock OL: 7 1/4" and 9 1/2". Courtesy of Emil and Martyl Pollak; 1983-207.

60

ENGLISH METAL PLANES

Some planes such as the tiny planes used by violin makers to shape the backs and bellies of their instruments had long been made of metal because it could be shaped more precisely than wood and was longer wearing. For the same reasons, English makers at the end of the century began to produce other planes made of iron, brass, or bronze. The smoothing plane (left) was made by an unknown maker, probably working in London during the early nineteenth century. The "miter" plane (ca. 1800, right), used to smooth end grain, and the bronze-bodied shave (early nineteenth century, below) were sold by one of several Green firms working in York, Sheffield, or London. During the nineteenth century, the manufacture of metal woodworking planes was brought to a high state of perfection, especially by the American toolmaking industry. OL: 7 1/2", 10 1/8", and 10 1/4". 1952-277, 75; 1991-616; 1992-116.

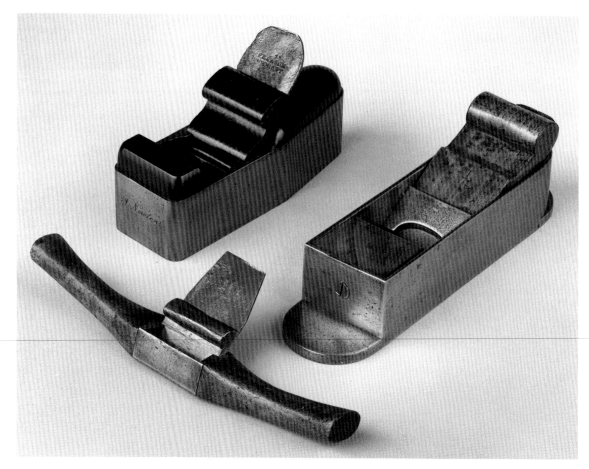

Afterword

Collecting old tools is a fast-growing hobby. Many books and periodicals that identify tools, explain how they were used, and relate the history of their makers are now available. A number of tool collectors' organizations also hold meetings, publish newsletters, and provide a variety of membership services.

Many woodworkers today buy old tools to use in their own shops. Their pleasing designs and good quality, coupled with the fact that many types of hand tools are no longer being manufactured, make them desirable additions to any woodworker's tool kit. It is important to remember, however, that tools are also important historical artifacts. While thousands of nineteenth-century tools survive, eighteenth-century tools are much rarer. Colonial Williamsburg is gradually discontinuing the use of original tools in its trade shops, replacing them with reproductions. The Foundation believes that it is our duty as a museum to preserve these important clues to the age of handwork. Williamsburg's choice may not be right for everyone, but these tools are a non-renewable, finite resource. When they are gone, there will be no more, and they are worthy of respect.

Some tools are valuable antiques with special appeal to collectors and museums because of their scarcity, historical importance, or the evidence of their use revealed in special modifications, sharpening, or even surface staining. Before cleaning and restoring an old tool, it is important to take the time to learn its history. How rare is it? What information can it, and maybe it alone, provide about early craftsmanship in America? Is it more important as an undisturbed historical artifact than as a newly polished and sharpened tool ready for use? Caring for old tools involves the same concerns as caring for other fine antiques. Certain cleaning methods or improper storage can, in the long run, do more harm than good. If you are a guardian of old tools, take the time to check with a museum or read a book such as *Caring for Your Collections* by Arthur W. Schultz (New York: H. N. Abrams, 1992) to determine how best to protect them so that they will continue to be around for your children and grandchildren.

81. An eighteenth-century paint or glue brush, once among the most common of artisans' tools, is today incredibly rare. This brush was found in the Mason House, Guilford, Virginia, in a location that indicates it was lost when the house was built about 1730. It is the only known surviving American example dating before 1800. L1992-90, loaned by Frank W. Blake II.

82. The fragile surfaces of tools often record the hands of the men who used them. 1991-102; 1991-562.

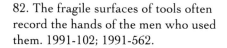

Notes

1. Matthew Carter, "British Planemakers Before 1700," in Emil Pollak and Martyl Pollak, eds., *Selections from The Chronicle: The Fascinating World of Early Tools and Trades* (Mendham, N. J., 1991), p. 348.

2. Alan Ferguson, "Collectors Cornered," *Tool and Trades History Society Newsletter*, VI (1984), p. 21.

3. By 1747, London warehousemen dealing in London, Sheffield, and Birmingham wares, including "all sorts of Tools," carried on "a very extensive Trade, and are reputed wealthy." T. Waller, *A General Description of All Trades* (London, 1747), p. 18.

4. Robert Campbell, *The London Tradesman. Being a Compendious View of All the Trades, Professions, Arts, both Liberal and Mechanic, now practised in the Cities of London and Westminster* (1747) (New York, 1969), pp. 240–241.

5. T. S. Willan, *The Early History of the Don Navigation*, in David Hey, *The Rural Metalworkers of the Sheffield Region: A Study of Rural Industry before the Industrial Revolution*, Department of English Local History, Occasional Papers, 2nd Ser. (Leicester, Eng., 1972), p. 53.

6. Thomas Hutton, *An Introduction to the Mechanical Part of Clock and Watch Work* (1773), in T. S. Ashton, *An Eighteenth-Century Industrialist: Peter Stubs of Warrington, 1756–1806* (New York, 1970), p. 2.

7. James Blair to [?], 1768, King's MS 206, British Museum, quoted in Harold B. Gill, Jr., "The Blacksmith in Colonial Virginia," research report, Oct. 1965, Colonial Williamsburg Foundation, p. 101.

8. Entry for June 9, 1789, William Allason Papers, Falmouth Store Daybook, June 20, 1777–Apr. 7, 1800, David and William Allason Business Records, Business Records Collection, Archives and Records Division, Virginia State Library and Archives, Richmond, Va.

9. He goes on to conclude: "I do not know that there is a whitesmith or maker of Cutlery in the Colony." Gov. Francis Fauquier to the Lords of Trade and Plantations, Dec. 17, 1766, C.O. 5/1331, fols. 162–163, Public Record Office, quoted in George H. Reese, ed., *The Official Papers of Francis Fauquier, Lieutenant Governor of Virginia, 1758–1768*, III (Charlottesville, Va., 1983), p. 1409.

10. Raleigh Downman to Messrs. Clay & Midgley, July 4, 1770, July 2, 1771, Joseph Ball and Raleigh Downman Letterbook, Library of Congress.

11. *Pennsylvania Chronicle* (Philadelphia), Mar. 2–9, 1767; Alan G. Bates, *Thomas Napier: The Scottish Connection* (n.p., 1986).

12. *Virginia Gazette* (Williamsburg) (Purdie), July 28, 1775.

13. *Pa. Chron.*, Sept. 12, 1734.

14. *Va. Gaz.* (Purdie and Dixon), Apr. 14, 1774.

15. *New-York Gazette*, Nov. 19, 1759, in Rita Susswein Gottesman, comp., *The Arts and Crafts in New York*. I: *1726–1776* (New York, 1938), pp. 197–198.

16. Gov. William Gooch to the Board of Trade, Dec. 22, 1731, C.O. 5/1322, fols. 219–221.

17. *The New-York Journal or General Advertiser*, Oct. 8, 1767, in Gottesman, comp., *Arts and Crafts in New York*, p. 209.

18. Copy of a Memorandum sent by Mr. Alexander, Oct. 31, 1779, Hagley Library, Greenville, Del.

19. Lee Richmond and Hampton Williams, "Planemakers of the 18C Shenandoah Valley," *Chronicle of the Early American Industries Association*, XLV (1992), pp. 112–113.

20. Advertisements for George Appleby (1748) and Cornelius Atherton (1770) in Gottesman, comp., *Arts and Crafts in New York*, pp. 290, 312.

21. Theodore R. Crom, *Trade Catalogues, 1542–1842* (Gainesville, Fla., 1989), p. 150.

22. Campbell, *London Tradesman*, pp. 171–172.

23. Susan Myra Kingsbury, ed., *The Records of the Virginia Company of London*, III (Washington, D. C., 1933), pp. 94–98, 178–189.

24. *For the Colony in Virginea Britannia. Lawes Diuine, Morall and Martiall, &c.* (1612), in Peter Force, comp., *Tracts and Other Papers, Relating Principally to the Origin, Settlement, and Progress of the Colonies in North America, From the Discovery of the Country to the Year 1776*, III (Gloucester, Mass., 1963), no. 2, pp. 13, 15.

25. "The Inconviencies That Have Happened to Some Persons Which Have Transported Themselves from England to Virginia" (1622), in W. L. Goodman, "The Virginia Company Broadside, 1622," *Chron. Early Amer. Ind. Assn.*, XXXIII (1980), p. 26.

26. *Va. Gaz.* (Purdie and Dixon), June 4, 1767.

27. Apprenticeship indenture of John Miller, Jan. 12, 1725/6, Lancaster County, Virginia, Order Book VII, 1721–1729, p. 150.

28. Apprenticeship indenture of John Garrow, Mar. 16, 1746/7, York County, Virginia, Deeds, V, 1741–1754, p. 208.

29. Apprenticeship Indenture of John Oen, Aug. 20, 1747, Fredericksville Parish, Louisa and Albemarle Counties, Pt. II, Indentures and Processioners' Returns, 1742–1787, pp. 23–24, Episcopal Church Records, Acc. 19765, Va. State Lib. and Arch.

30. John Parish judgment, Mar. 8, 1726/7, Lancaster Co. Recs., Order Book VII, p. 229.

31. 1 pound = 20 shillings = 240 pence. Harold B. Gill, "Prices and Wages in 1750," research memorandum, Sept. 1977, CWF, p. 3.

32. John Glassford and Company Records for Virginia, Boyd's Hole Store, Ledger 3, 1769–1770, fol. 5, Lib. Cong.

33. *Ibid.*, Colchester Store, Ledger Book D, 1763–1764, fols. 175, 226; Ledger Book E, 1765, fols. 10, 11, 145,

152; Ledger Book F, 1766, fols. 97, 113; Ledger Book G, 1766–1767, fol. 97.

34. Invoice of Joiners Tools Vizt from James Bowie [May 31, 1768], Invoice and Inventory Book for Falmouth Store, 1767–1769, p. 13; Ledger F, Oct. 1767–Sept. 1768, p. 29, Allason Business Recs.

35. *Va. Gaz.,* Sept. 12, 1755.

36. Will of John McCloud, Jan. 14, 1795, Petersburg Hustings Court, Will Book I, 1784–1805, pp. 231–232, in Jonathan Prown, "A Cultural Analysis of Furniture-making in Petersburg, Virginia, 1760–1820," *Journal of Early Southern Decorative Arts,* XVIII (1992), p. 130.

37. Will of Charles Grim, Aug. 16, 1777, Frederick County, Virginia, Will Book IV, pp. 391–392.

38. *Va. Gaz.* (Dixon and Hunter), Mar. 9, 1776.

39. Hugh Jones, *The Present State of Virginia,* ed. Richard L. Morton (Chapel Hill, N. C., 1956), p. 76.

40. John Christian Kolbe, "Thomas Elfe, Eighteenth Century Charleston Cabinetmaker" (M.A. thesis, University of South Carolina, 1980), p. 28; Charles Hummel, personal correspondence.

41. Benno M. Forman, "Delaware Valley 'Crookt Foot' and Slat-Back Chairs: The Fussell-Savery Connection," *Winterthur Portfolio,* XV (1980), p. 45.

42. Eileen Yeo and E. P. Thompson, *The Unknown Mayhew* (New York, 1972), p. 347.

43. *Virginia Centinel; or, The Winchester Mercury,* July 9, 1788.

44. David Pye, *The Nature and Art of Workmanship* (Cambridge, 1968), pp. 4–6.

45. Benno M. Forman, *American Seating Furniture 1630–1730: An Interpretive Catalogue* (New York, 1988), pp. 47, 49, 372; Invoice of Sundries to be Sent by Robert Cary and Company for Use of George Washington [Sept. 1759], John C. Fitzpatrick, ed., *The Writings of George Washington from the Original Manuscript Sources, 1745–1799.* II: *1757–1769* (Washington, D. C., 1931), p. 333; Charles F. Hummel, "English Tools in America: The Evidence of the Dominys," *Winterthur Port.,* II (1965), p. 28.

46. W. L. Goodman, "Gabriel & Sons, Stock Inventories," *Chron. Early Amer. Ind. Assn.,* XXXVI (1983), pp. 58–61.

47. Duplicate of an Invoice of Goods by Couzzins to be sent Robert Beverley at Blanfield in Virginia, 1763, Robert Beverley Letterbook, 1761–1775, Lib. Cong.

48. Ken Hawley, "Getting Their Own Back," *Tool and Trades Hist. Soc. Newsletter,* XXXVI (1992), pp. 24–25.

Notes

Glossary

This glossary includes only technical terms used frequently in this book. For a comprehensive presentation of woodworking tool terms and descriptions, see R. A. Salaman, *Dictionary of Woodworking Tools, c. 1700–1970, and Tools of the Allied Trades*, rev. ed. (Newtown, Conn., 1990).

ADZE: A tool with a blade set across the line of the handle, like a hoe. The poll, or end of the head opposite the cutting edge, is often in the form of a hammer or pin for striking or driving. Adzes were used to smooth hewn wood and chop curved surfaces to shape.

AUGER: A tool for boring large holes. Augers usually were attached to a wooden T handle by which they were turned into the work. See page 89.

AX: A tool for chopping or paring. Axes were made in many different shapes for cutting down trees (felling axes), hewing them to shape (broad axes), and performing a variety of specialized chopping and paring tasks (wheelwrights', joiners', and coopers' axes).

BENCH PLANES: Planes used to reduce wood to the desired thickness, make it straight, and smooth its surfaces. See page 96.

BEVEL: A tool with two arms that can be set at an angle and used to gauge that angle or transfer it to another workpiece. See page 69.

BIT: A tool for boring holes, usually fitted to a brace or some other form of drill. See pages 92–93.

BOLSTER: A shoulder forged on the shank of tanged tools that prevents their handles from sliding forward. See page 71.

BRACE: A tool using the crank principle to impart a continuous turning motion to a boring or shaping bit. Also known as piercers, wimbles, and bitstocks. See pages 91–94.

BRAD AWL: A tool resembling a small chisel or screwdriver but used instead to create small holes. See page 91.

BRASSES: Handles and other cabinet hardware usually made of cast brass.

CABINETMAKER: A woodworker who made furniture consisting of fitted cases such as chests-of-drawers, desks, clothespresses, and clock cases. In eighteenth-century America, cabinetmaking frequently was combined with chairmaking, turning, and joiner's work.

CALIPERS: A tool similar to compasses (see below) except that its legs are curved so that their points can be brought to bear on curved objects. See page 68.

CARVING TOOLS: Chisels and gouges made in special shapes for executing decorative carving. See page 77.

CAST IRON: Iron produced directly by smelting ore in a blast furnace. Although it can be cast into various shapes, including pots, kettles, and cannon, it contains too many impurities and too much carbon for it to be of use for most toolmaking. It is the material from which wrought iron and steel, both used extensively for toolmaking, were made.

CHISEL: A tool with a flat blade, sharpened on its end, for paring and chopping. There were two methods of mounting wooden handles onto chisels. Some had their handles mounted onto small pins or tangs projecting from the back of the tool. The backs of others were made as hollow sockets into which the handle fit. See pages 71–72.

CLAMP: A device, often made of wood, for holding parts together while they were being assembled. Clamps were used most frequently for positioning pieces while glue dried. See page 9.

COMPASSES: A tool that is often called a "pair of dividers" today. It consists of two legs hinged at the top so that the ends of the legs can be set apart at a desired distance. See page 68.

COOPER: A tradesman who produced barrel-like containers consisting of bound staves, including barrels, hogsheads, kegs, pails, churns, and tubs.

CUTLERY: Knives, razors, scissors, and other edged implements. The manufacture of cutlery and edge tools were distinct trades.

DADO: A groove across the width of a board, usually across the grain.

DEPTH STOP: A device on a plane or other tool that stops the tool's cutting action at a given depth.

DOVETAIL JOINT: A method of joining boards together by interlocking, triangular projections.

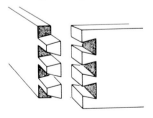

DOWELING: Assembling wood by inserting round pegs into holes drilled in the pieces to be joined. This technique was used most frequently by coopers to form the ends of their containers.

DRAWKNIFE: A narrow blade, sharpened along one side, with handles mounted on each end. It pares wood as the user draws the tool toward him. Specialized types with curved blades were used by coopers and others for forming concave surfaces. See page 40.

EDGE TOOL: A tool with a sharpened cutting edge, including axes, adzes, chisels, boring tools, and various blades.

FENCE: A device on a plane or gauge that rides along the edge of the work, properly positioning the tool.

FERRULE: A ring, usually made of metal, placed around a piece of wood to keep it from splitting.

FORGE: A workshop where iron and steel are hammered to shape. Forges for making large iron products often had hammers powered by waterwheels. FORGING is the process of hammering metal to the desired shape.

GAUGE: Most commonly in woodworking, a tool for marking or cutting a parallel line a set distance from the edge of a workpiece. Most gauges consist of a stem upon which an adjustable fence (see above) is mounted. As the user runs the fence along the edge of the work, one or more pins or blades mounted on the end of the stem score or cut the desired line(s). See page 66.

GIMLET: A tool, resembling a small auger, for boring holes. See page 90.

GOUGE: A chisel-like tool with a blade curved from side to side. See page 73.

GRINDING: The process of finishing tools or shaping their cutting edges preparatory to sharpening them by holding them against a rapidly turning abrasive wheel. The most common wheels were made of sandstone. Individual woodworkers often owned small hand-powered grindstones for maintaining their tools. Tool manufacturers used large wheels, often driven by waterpower.

INLAY: Small pieces of wood set into the surface of a product, usually for their decorative effect.

IRON: Wrought iron was the material forged by blacksmiths and toolmakers into hardware and implements. It contains less carbon than steel and cannot be hardened, so many tools consisted of an iron body with a welded-on steel edge. (See CAST IRON and STEEL.) Plane blades are called "irons."

IRONMONGER: The English term for a merchant who sold hardware of various types, including tools.

JIG: Any one of an almost infinite variety of devices that holds a workpiece in the proper position in relation to a tool being used to shape it. Many jigs also control the action of the tool. A common example is a miter box, which automatically positions a saw to make a forty-five-degree cut. Most woodworking trades used one or more specialized jigs, often homemade.

JOINER: Strictly defined, a joiner was a woodworker who undertook architectural finishing work such as the making of doors, windows, and paneling. Carpenters built the basic structure including walls, roof, and floors. In practice, these trades often were combined. Seventeenth-century furniture makers, who used woodworking techniques similar to those employed in house finishing, also were called joiners, and in eighteenth-century America, cabinetmakers often called themselves joiners.

JOINING PLANES: Planes used to cut steps, grooves, tongues, and other interlocking shapes for joining wooden pieces. See page 104.

LATHE: A machine that spins a piece of wood while a turner holds chisels or gouges against it to cut it to shape. Some lathes were foot powered. Others were powered by a large wheel turned by an assistant. See pages 49 and 57.

LAYOUT TOOLS: Laying-out is the process of marking wood to be cut to a desired shape. Layout tools such as squares, bevels, and gauges are devices that ease this task and increase the accuracy of the process.

LEVELS and PLUMBS: Devices for determining whether surfaces are respectively horizontal or vertical. Most consisted of a plumb bob suspended on a wooden mount. When the edge of the mount was held against a level or vertical surface, the bob's string hung along a scribed line. See page 45.

MILLWRIGHT: An artisan who made and assembled the wooden machinery of gristmills, sawmills, and other heavy powered devices.

MOLDING PLANES: Planes used to cut decorative shapes on the edges or surfaces of wood. See pages 98–99.

MORTISE-AND-TENON JOINT: A method of joining wood by creating a rectangular tongue on one piece that fit into a corresponding slot in the other.

PANEL: A thin, flat piece of wood held in place by a surrounding framework. Eighteenth-century panels often have tapered edges that fit into a groove along the inside of the frame. If the tapering shows on the front of the panel, the central, flat area is called the field. Panel-raising planes cut the taper and leave a well-defined field.

PARING: The process of cutting away thin slivers or shavings of wood with an edge tool.

PATTERNS: Wood, metal, or paper devices shaped to a form to be reproduced. The task of laying out work was much simplified if it could be traced from an existing pattern, and many woodworkers developed a whole range of patterns suited to the production of their wares.

PINCERS: Gripping tools used most frequently by woodworkers for pulling nails and brads. See page 5.

PITSAW: A long, two-man saw used to saw logs lengthwise into boards. See page 81.

PLANE: A tool consisting of a chisel-like blade mounted in a wooden body or stock that was pushed over the work to cut it to the desired size or shape or to smooth its surfaces.

RABBET: A step on the edge of a board.

RULE: A ruler, most commonly with one or more joints that allowed it to be folded. Typical eighteenth-century rules were two feet long. See page 65.

SCRAPER: A thin piece of steel or glass used to smooth a surface by scraping. Steel scrapers made in appropriate shapes were used to create moldings in situations where planes were impractical, such as the molded edges of "pie-crust" tables.

SPOKESHAVE: A tool consisting of a wooden body with handles formed at each end and a blade mounted to its bottom. The body helps control the angle and depth of cut. See page 28, lower right.

SQUARE: A tool consisting of two arms joined at a right angle for marking and testing pieces that need to be "square." See pages 64 and 66.

STEEL: Iron containing small amounts of carbon that transform it into a material that can be brought to various degrees of hardness by heating and cooling. To be effective, the cutting edges of tools have to be made of steel rather than iron. Steel was shaped by forging.

STOCK: The wooden body of a plane. See page 96.

TANG: A projecting piece of metal over which a handle is mounted. See page 71.

TONGUE-AND-GROOVE JOINT: A method of joining boards edge-to-edge by creating a tongue on the edge of one that fit into a groove on the edge of the other.

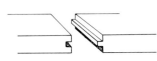

TURNER: A woodworker who made products by turning them on a lathe.

VENEER: Thin pieces of wood applied to the surface of woodwork for their decorative effect.

WHEELWRIGHT: A woodworker who made vehicles including their wheels and other mechanical components. Coachmakers specialized in more refined vehicles for personal transportation, while chairmakers made lightweight, open vehicles called "riding chairs."

Glossary

Further Reading

The following publications contain information about early tools and their makers and users. They have been selected because they should be available either for purchase or through major libraries. Many contain extensive bibliographies that will guide the reader to additional sources. Also of interest, but not included in this list, are books about cabinetmakers and joiners and their work, architecture, and other specific woodworking trades and their products. Many of them contain fascinating details of tool kits and their use. The reader is also advised to consult the publications of the many tool collecting groups in the United States and Canada and the Tool and Trades History Society in England.

Bates, Alan G. *Thomas Napier: The Scottish Connection.* N.p.: Early American Industries Association and the Mid-West Tool Collectors Association, 1986.

Barraclough, K. C. *Sheffield Steel.* Derbyshire, Eng.: Moorland Publishing Co. Ltd. for Sheffield City Museums, 1976.

Campbell, Robert. *The London Tradesman. Being a Compendious View of All the Trades, Professions, Arts, both Liberal and Mechanic, now practised in the Cities of London and Westminster.* London, 1747. Reprint. New York: Augustus M. Kelley, 1969.

Catalogue of Measuring Rules, Tapes, Straight Edges, and Steel Band Chains; Spirit Levels, &c. Manufactured by John Rabone & Sons. Birmingham, Eng., 1892. Reprint. Introduced and edited by Kenneth D. Roberts. Fitzwilliam, N. H.: Ken Roberts Publishing Co., 1982.

Crom, Theodore R. *Trade Catalogues, 1542–1842.* Melrose, Fla.: T. R. Crom, 1989.

Dane, E. Surrey. *Peter Stubs and the Lancashire Hand Tool Industry.* Altrincham, Eng.: John Sherratt and Son Ltd., 1973.

Diderot, Denis. *Recueil de planches, sur les sciences, les arts liberaux, et les arts mechaniques, avec leur explication* [Pictorial Encyclopedia of Science, Art, and Technology]. Paris, 1762. Reprint. New York: Readex Microprint Corporation, 1969. (In French only.)

Garvin, James L., and Donna-Belle Garvin. *Instruments of Change: New Hampshire Hand Tools and Their Makers, 1800–1900.* Canaan, N. H.: Phoenix Publishing for the New Hampshire Historical Society, 1985.

Goodman, W. L. *British Planemakers from 1700.* 3rd ed. Rev. by Jane and Mark Rees. Needham Market, Eng.: Roy Arnold, 1993.

_____. *History of Woodworking Tools.* London: G. Bell, 1964.

Hey, David. "The Origins and Early Growth of the Hallamshire Cutlery and Allied Trades." In *English Rural Society, 1500–1800: Essays in Honour of Joan Thirsk,* edited by John Chartres and David Hey, pp. 343–367. Cambridge: Cambridge University Press, 1990.

Hindle, Brooke, ed. *America's Wooden Age: Aspects of its Early Technology.* Tarrytown, N. Y.: Sleepy Hollow Restorations, 1975.

Hummel, Charles F. "English Tools in America: The Evidence of the Dominys." *Winterthur Portfolio,* II (1965), pp. 27–46.

_____. *With Hammer in Hand: The Dominy Craftsmen of East Hampton, New York.* Charlottesville, Va.: University Press of Virginia for the Henry Francis du Pont Winterthur Museum, 1968.

Kauffman, Henry J. *American Axes: A Survey of Their Development and Their Makers.* Brattleboro, Vt.: Stephen Greene Press, 1972.

Kean, Herbert P., and Emil S. Pollak. *Collecting Antique Tools.* Morristown, N. J.: Astragal Press, 1990.

Kebabian, Paul B. *American Woodworking Tools.* Boston: New York Graphic Society, 1978.

Kebabian, Paul B., and William C. Lipke, eds. *Tools and Technologies: America's Wooden Age.* Burlington, Vt.: Robert Hull Fleming Museum, University of Vermont, 1979.

Landis, Scott. *The Workbench Book.* Newtown, Conn.: Taunton Press, 1987.

_____. *The Workshop Book.* Newtown, Conn.: Taunton Press, 1991.

Longenecker, Elmer Z. "The Early Blacksmiths of Lancaster County [Pennsylvania]." *Community Historians Annual,* X. Lancaster, Pa.: Schaff Library, Lancaster Theological Seminary, 1971.

Mercer, Henry Chapman. *Ancient Carpenters' Tools: Illustrated and Explained, Together with the Implements of the Lumberman, Joiner, and Cabinet Maker, in Use in the Eighteenth Century.* Reprint. Doylestown, Pa.: Bucks County Historical Society, 1960.

Moxon, Joseph. *Mechanick Exercises: or, The Doctrine of Handy-works.* 3rd ed. London, 1703. Reprint. Morristown, N. J.: Astragal Press, 1989.

Pollak, Emil, and Martyl Pollak. *Guide to American Wooden Planes and Their Makers.* 2nd ed. Morristown, N. J.: Astragal Press, 1987.

Pollak, Emil, and Martyl Pollak, eds. *Selections from The Chronicle: The Fascinating World of Early Tools and Trades.* Mendham, N. J.: Astragal Press, 1991.

Proudfoot, Christopher, and Philip Walker. *Woodworking Tools.* Rutland, Vt.: C. E. Tuttle Co., 1984.

Pye, David. *The Nature and Art of Workmanship.* Cambridge: Cambridge University Press, 1968.

Roberts, Kenneth D. *Some Nineteenth-Century English Woodworking Tools: Edge and Joiner Tools and Bit Braces.* Fitzwilliam, N. H.: Ken Roberts Publishing Co., 1980.

_____. *Tools for the Trades and Crafts: An Eighteenth Century Pattern Book, R. Timmins & Sons, Birmingham.* Fitzwilliam, N. H.: Ken Roberts Publishing Co., 1976.

Roberts, Kenneth D., and Jane W. Roberts. *Planemakers and Other Edge Tool Enterprises in New York State in the Nineteenth Century.* Cooperstown, N. Y.: New York State Historical Society and Early American Industries Association, 1971.

Rowlands, Marie B. "Continuity and Change in an Industrialising Society: The Case of the West Midlands Industries." In *Regions and Industries: A Perspective on the Industrial Revolution in Britain,* edited by Pat Hudson, pp. 103–131. New York: Cambridge University Press, 1989.

_____. *Masters and Men in the West Midlands Metalware Trades before the Industrial Revolution.* Manchester, Eng.: Manchester University Press, 1975.

Salaman, R. A. *Dictionary of Woodworking Tools, c. 1700–1970, and Tools of the Allied Trades.* Rev. ed. Newtown, Conn.: Taunton Press, 1990.

Schultz, Arthur W. *Caring for Your Collections: Art and Other Collectibles.* National Committee to Save America's Cultural Collections. New York: H. N. Abrams, 1992.

Sellens, Alvin, comp. *Dictionary of American Hand Tools: A Pictorial Synopsis.* Augusta, Kans.: A. Sellens, 1990.

Semel, Daniel M. *Thomas Grant, Ironmonger.* N.p.: Early American Industries Association, 1978.

Sloane, Eric. *Museum of Early American Tools.* New York: W. Funk, 1964.

Smith, Joseph. *Explanation or Key, to the Various Manufactories of Sheffield, with Engravings of Each Article.* Edited by John S. Kebabian. South Burlington, Vt.: Early American Industries Association, 1975.

Stockham, Peter, ed. *Little Book of Early American Crafts and Trades.* Richmond, Va., 1807. Reprint. New York: Dover Publications, 1976.

Underhill, Roy. *The Woodwright's Companion: Exploring Traditional Woodcraft.* Chapel Hill, N. C.: University of North Carolina Press, 1983.

_____. *The Woodwright's Workbook.* Chapel Hill, N. C.: University of North Carolina Press, 1986.

Welsh, Peter C. *Woodworking Tools, 1600–1900.* Contributions from the Museum of History and Technology, Paper 51. Washington, D. C.: Smithsonian Institution, 1966.

Whelan, John M. *The Wooden Plane: Its History, Form, and Function.* Mendham, N. J.: Astragal Press, 1993.

Wyke, John. *Catalogue of Tools for Watch and Clock Makers.* Charlottesville, Va.: University Press of Virginia for the Henry Francis du Pont Winterthur Museum, 1978.

Journals

Chronicle of the Early American Industries Association.

The Gristmill. The publication of the Mid-West Tool Collectors Association.

Historic Trades Annual. Colonial Williamsburg Foundation.

Plane Talk. (No longer published, but back issues are available through Astragal Press, Mendham, N. J.)

Tools and Trades. The journal of the Tool and Trades History Society, England. They also publish a quarterly newsletter.

Index